Konrad Gesner

BEASTS & ANIMALS

in Decorative Woodcuts of the Renaissance

EDITED BY
Carol Belanger Grafton

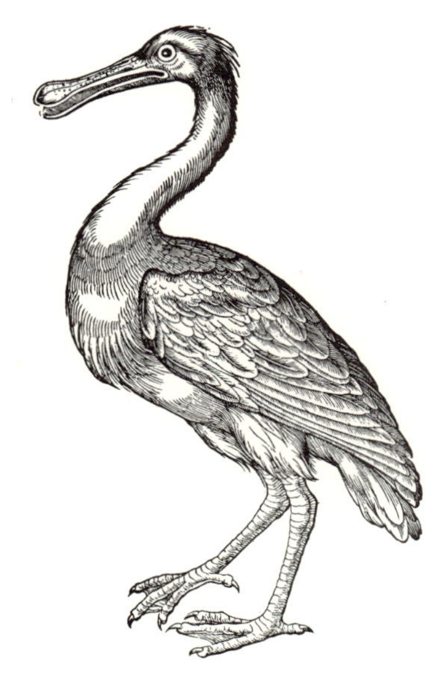

DOVER PUBLICATIONS, INC.
NEW YORK

Publisher's Note

This is the second collection of Renaissance animal illustrations published by Dover. The first, *Curious Woodcuts of Fanciful and Real Beasts* (1971, 22701-4), contains 190 cuts chosen for their decorative interest. The present volume brings together 271 more illustrations from the natural histories of Konrad Gesner (1516–1565) and Edward Topsell (d. 1638?).

Gesner, a Zurich-born physician and scholar, wrote extensively on many subjects. His four-volume *Historia Animalium,* the primary source of the art in this book, was first published in his native city between 1551 and 1563. Gesner collated the zoological writings of classical and medieval authors and added contemporary observations and reports on animals. His encyclopedic text was adorned with hundreds of woodcuts, some borrowed from colleagues near and far, others cut expressly for the *Historia.*

So vigorous were the illustrations that Gesner's publisher brought out pictorial volumes with brief captions (the *Icones*) during the decade of production of the *Historia.* The latter was reprinted several times, and versions of the same cuts were used in seventeenth-century England by Topsell, whose *History of Four-footed Beasts* provided the illustrations of all of the insects and some of the higher animals in the present compendium.

The pictures are generally arranged according to broad categories of modern taxonomy: mammals, birds, reptiles, fish, other sea creatures (including molluscs, crustaceans and echinoderms) and insects, with imaginary creatures at the end. For the most part, denizens of the Old World are depicted. The captions provide modern names in most cases, although some identifications are tentative. There is an Index of Animals at the end of the volume.

The publisher gratefully acknowledges the assistance of the staff of the American Museum of Natural History in New York. The reader is referred to the Publisher's Note in *Curious Woodcuts* for a more detailed history of the source materials and an appreciation of the iconography.

Published in Canada by General Publishing Company, Ltd., 30 Lesmill Road, Don Mills, Toronto, Ontario.
Published in the United Kingdom by Constable and Company, Ltd.

Beasts & Animals in Decorative Woodcuts of the Renaissance is a new selection of illustrations from the following works of Konrad Gesner: *Historiae Animalium Liber III. qui est de Avium natura* . . . , 2nd edition, Frankfurt, Robertus Cambierus, 1585; *Icones Avium Omnium* . . . , 2nd edition, Zurich, C[hristoph.] Froschoverus, 1560; *Nomenclator Aquatilium Animantium. Icones Animalium Aquatilium* . . . , Zurich, Christoph. Froschoverus, 1560; *Historiae Animalium Liber IV. Qui est de Piscium* . . . , 2nd edition, Frankfurt, Andreas Cambierus, 1604; as well as Edward Topsel[l]'s *The History of Four-footed Beasts and Serpents . . . Whereunto is now Added, The Theater of Insects . . . By T. Muffet* [Moffett], London, G. Sawbridge, T. Williams and T. Johnson, 1658.
The picture selection and layout are by Carol Belanger Grafton. The Publisher's Note, captions (based on the original texts) and Index of Animals were prepared specially for this edition by Joseph Cahn.

DOVER *Pictorial Archive* SERIES

Manufactured in the United States of America
Dover Publications, Inc., 31 East 2nd Street, Mineola, N.Y. 11501

Library of Congress Cataloging in Publication Data

Gesner, Konrad, 1516–1565.
Beasts & animals in decorative woodcuts of the Renaissance.

(Dover pictorial archive series)
Includes index.
1. Gesner, Konrad, 1516–1565. 2. Bestiaries in Art. 3. Animals in art. I. Title. II. Series.
NE1150.5.G47A4 1983 769'.432'094 82-17756
ISBN 0-486-24430-X

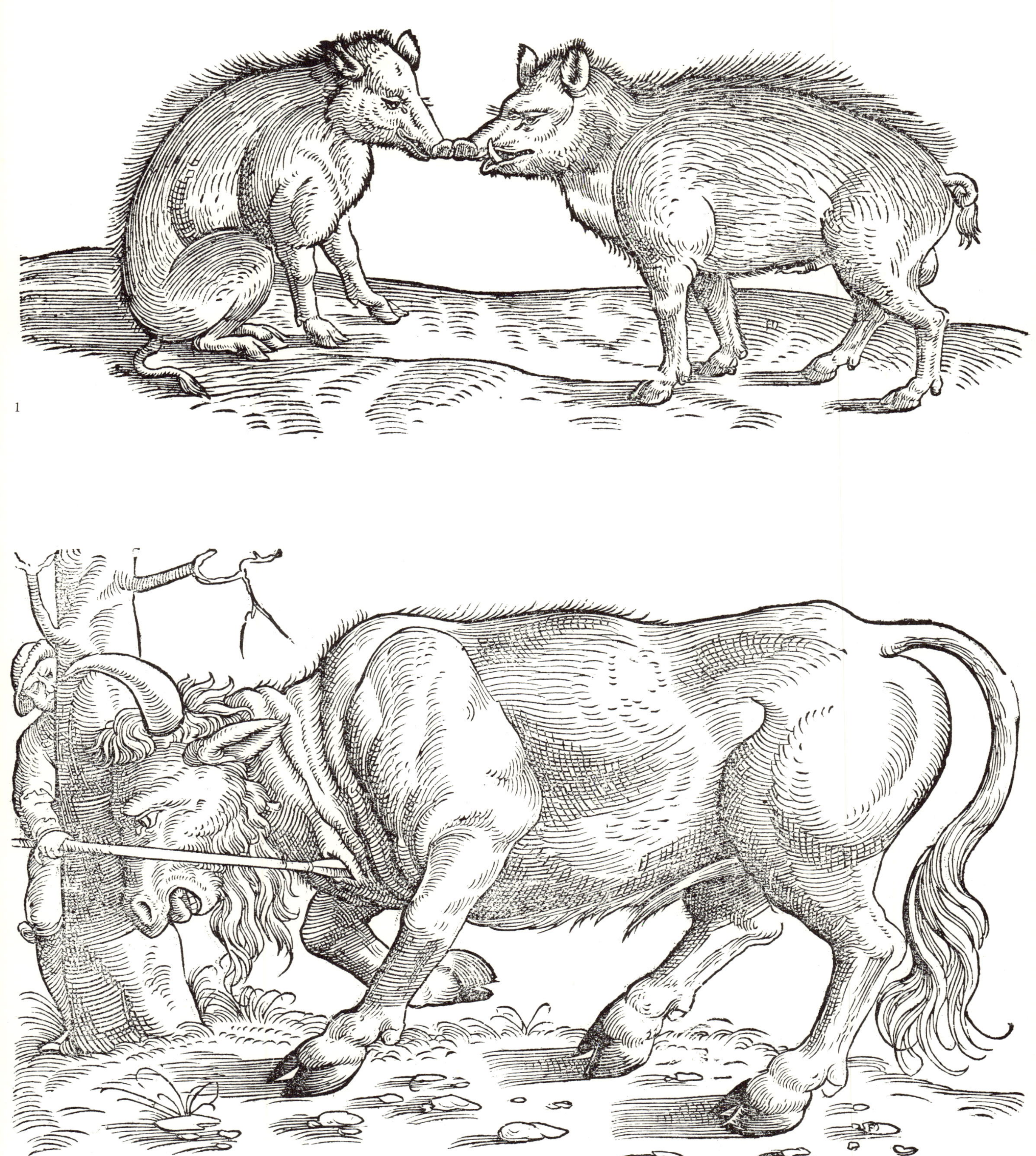

1. Swine (sow and boar). 2. Aurochs (a type of wild ox).

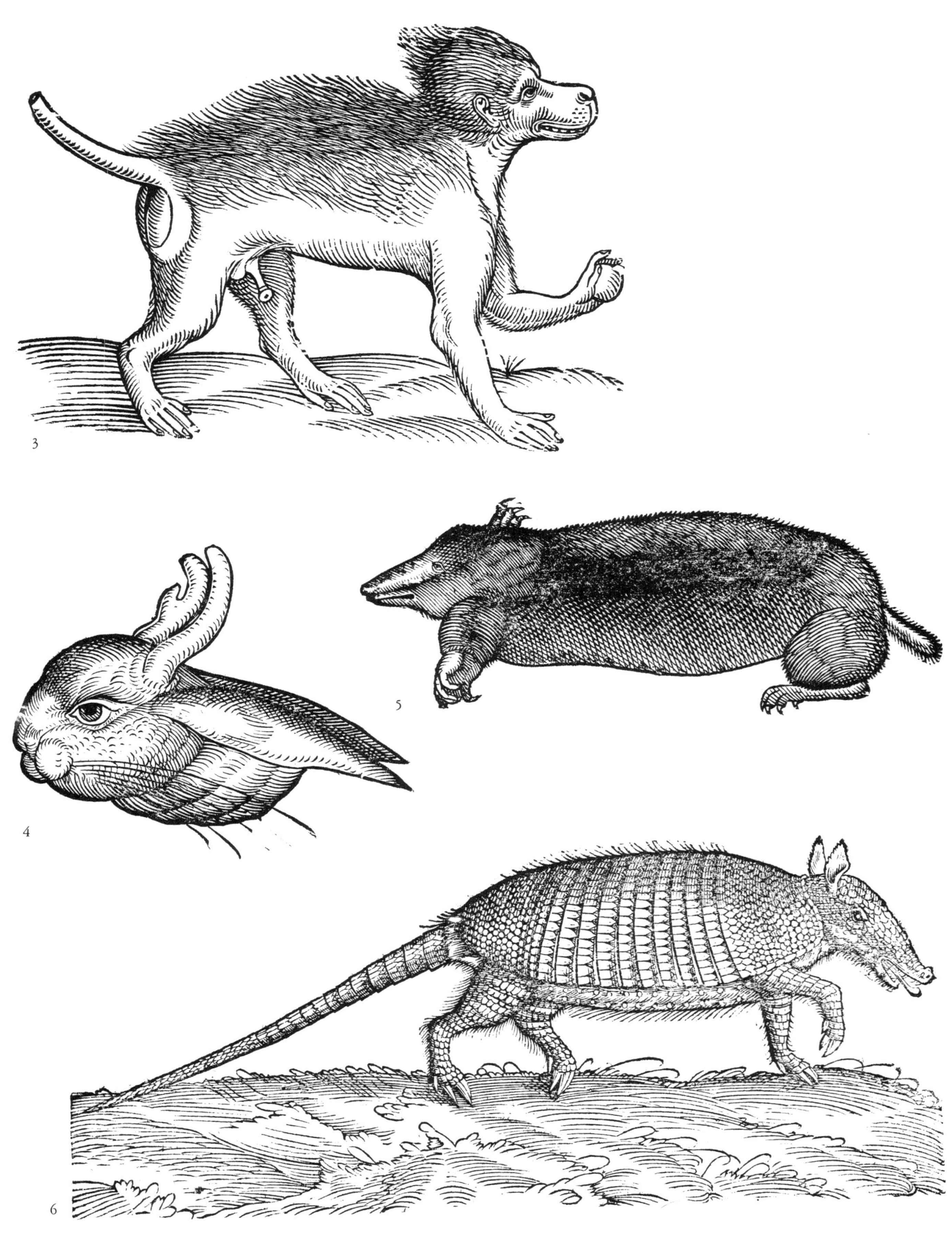

3. Baboon. 4. A horned hare reputed to live in Saxony. 5. Mole. 6. Armadillo.

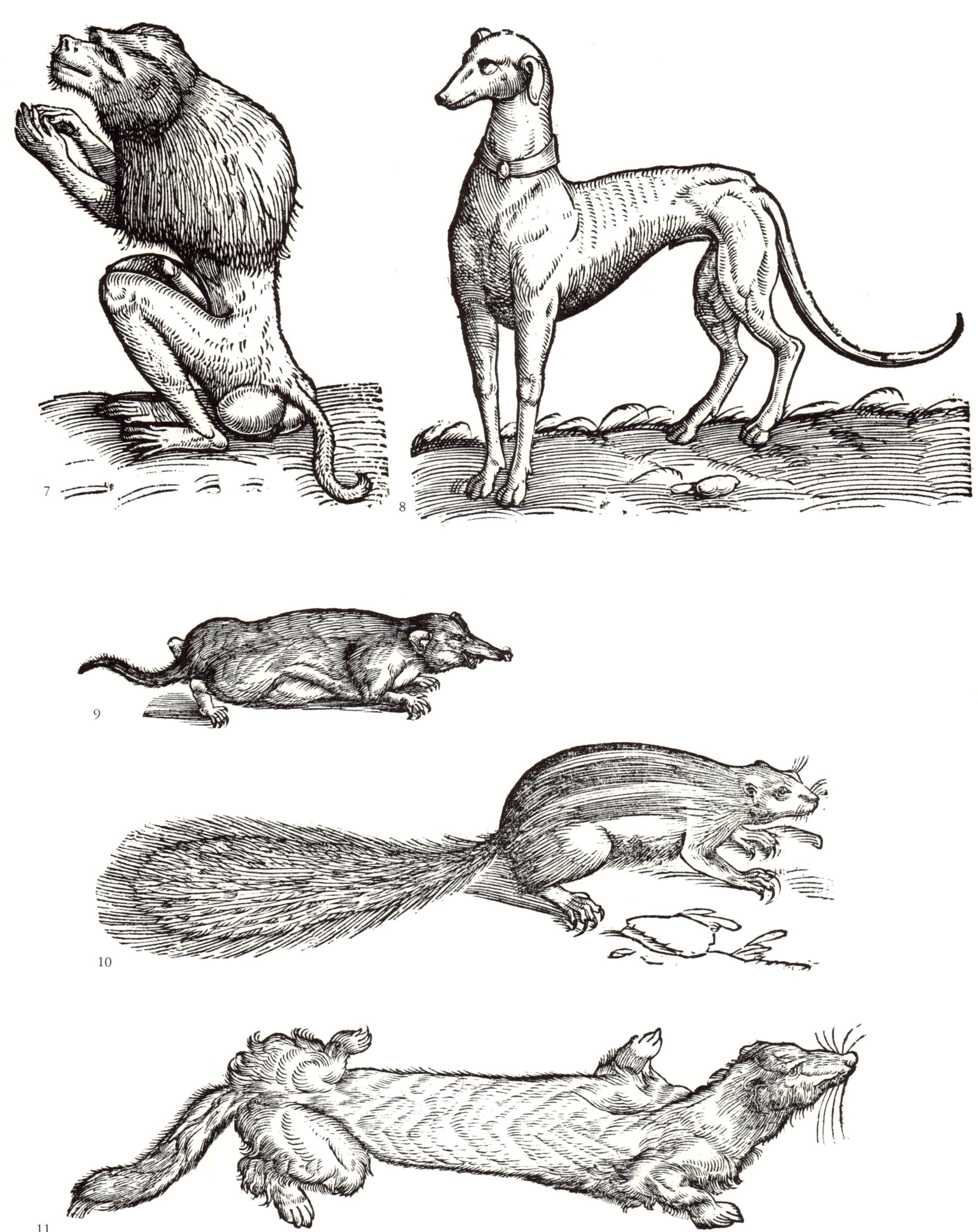

7. Another baboon or mandrill. 8. Greyhound. 9. Shrew. 10. Squirrel. 11. An Italian weasel.

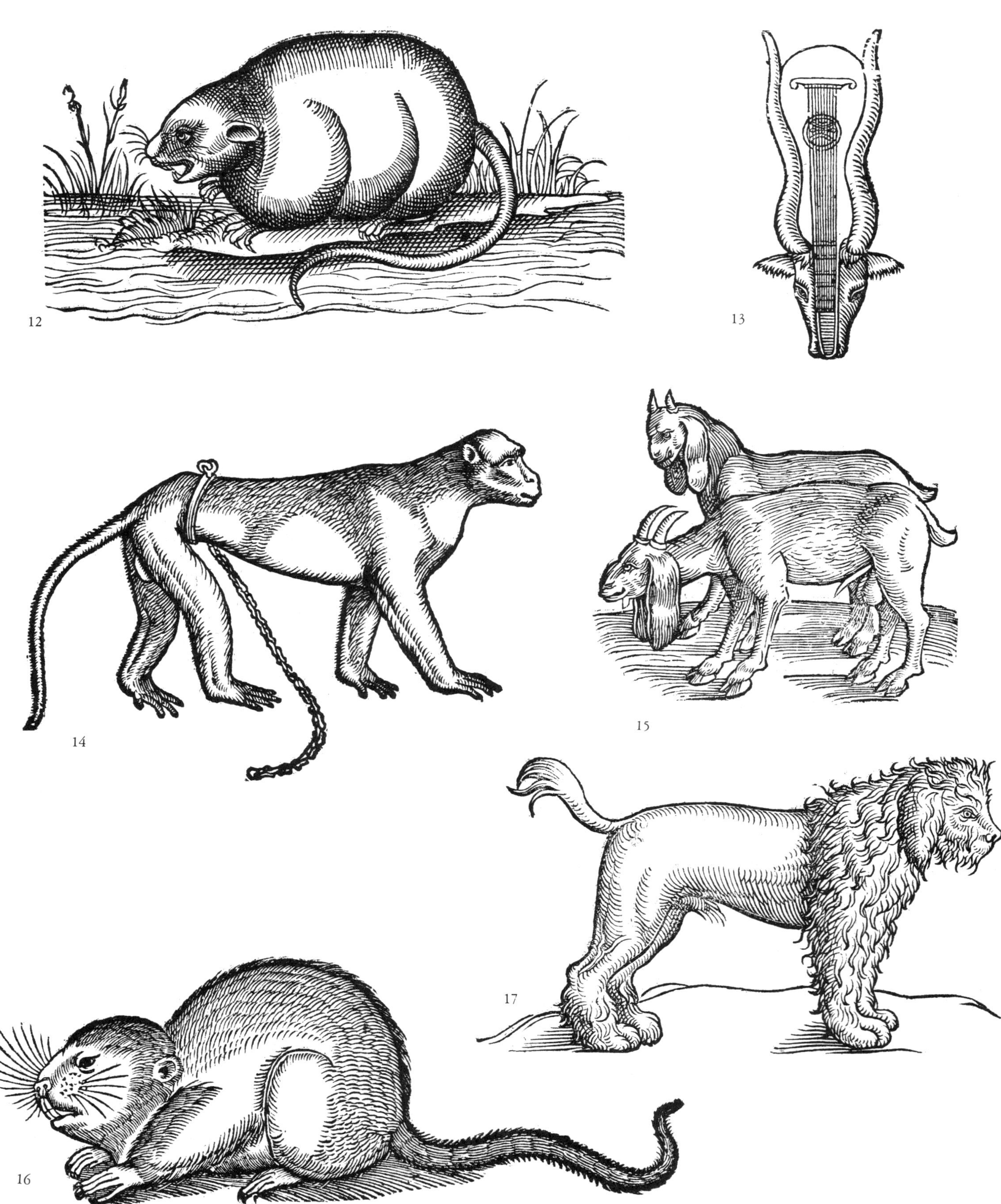

12. River rat. 13. Head of a Cretan sheep with a stringed instrument drawn in to show the curve of the horns. 14. A long-tailed monkey. 15. Indian goat. 16. Wild rat. 17. Water spaniel (ancestor of the poodle).

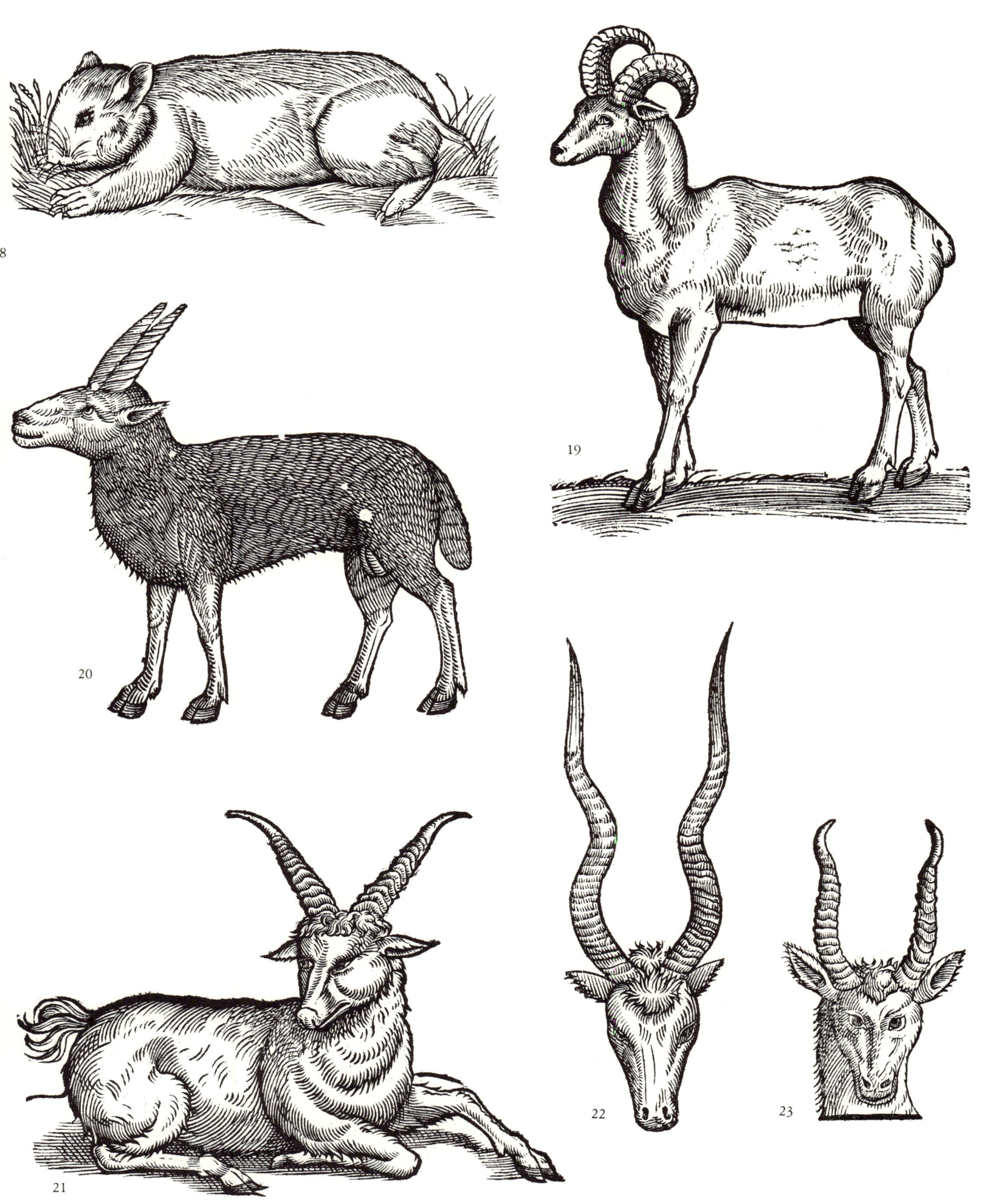

18. Hamster. 19. Mouflon (a type of wild sheep). 20. A type of sheep from Crete, probably the Walachian sheep. 21. Saiga (a sheep-like antelope of Central Asia). 22. Head of Cretan sheep. 23. Head of saiga.

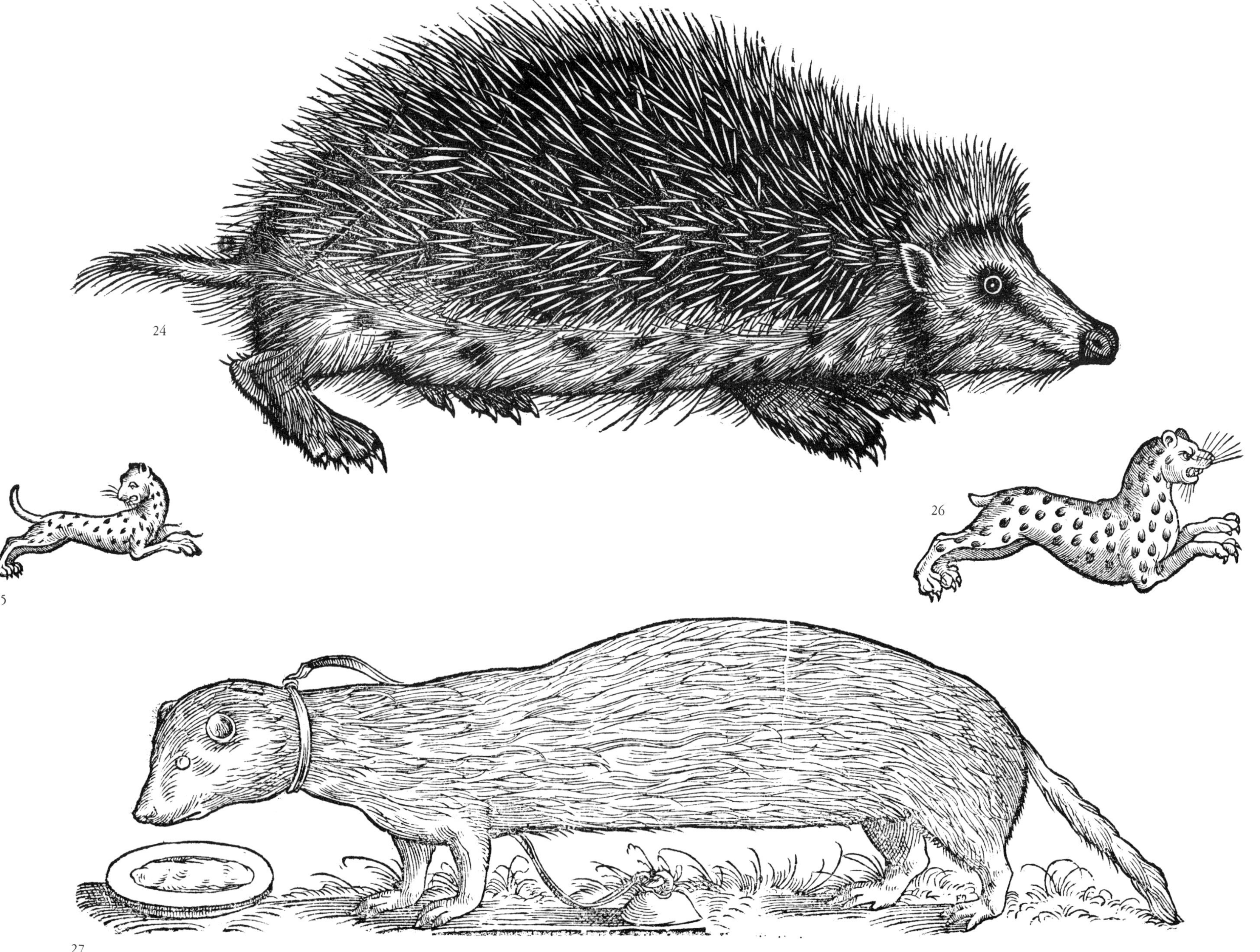

24. Hedgehog. 25 and 26. Wild cats. 27. Ferret.

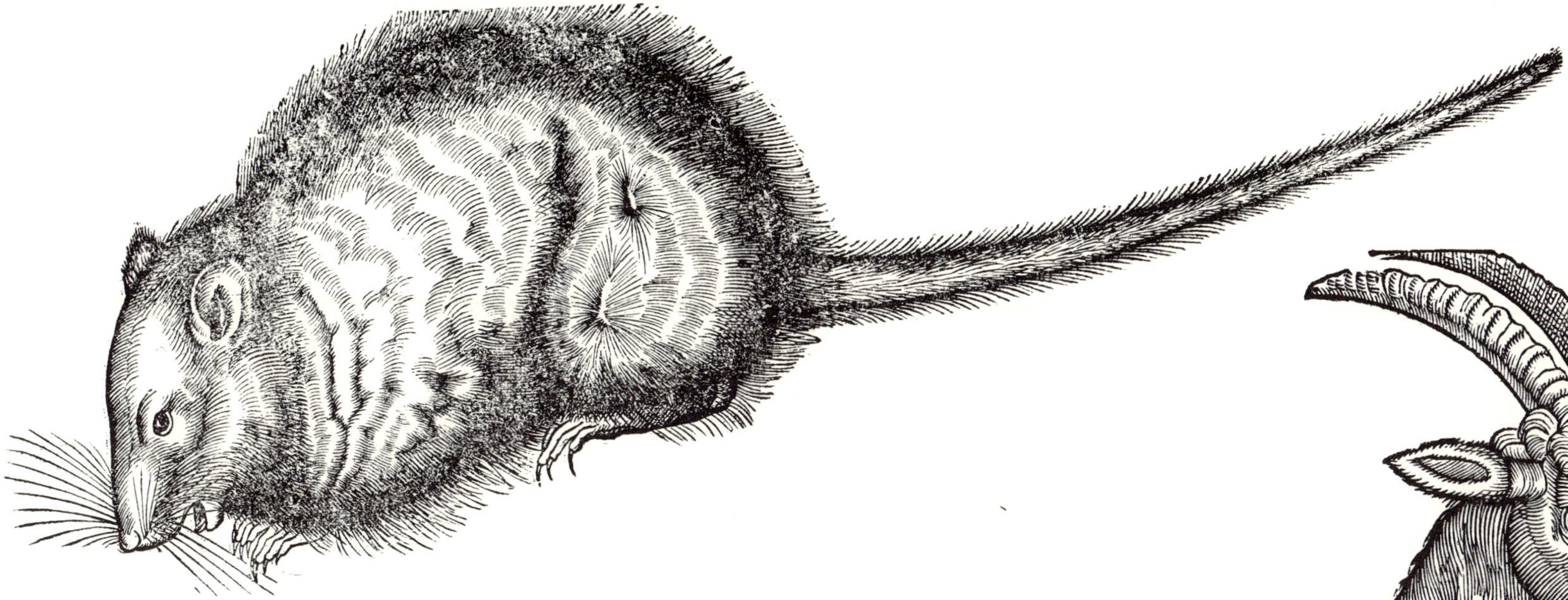

28

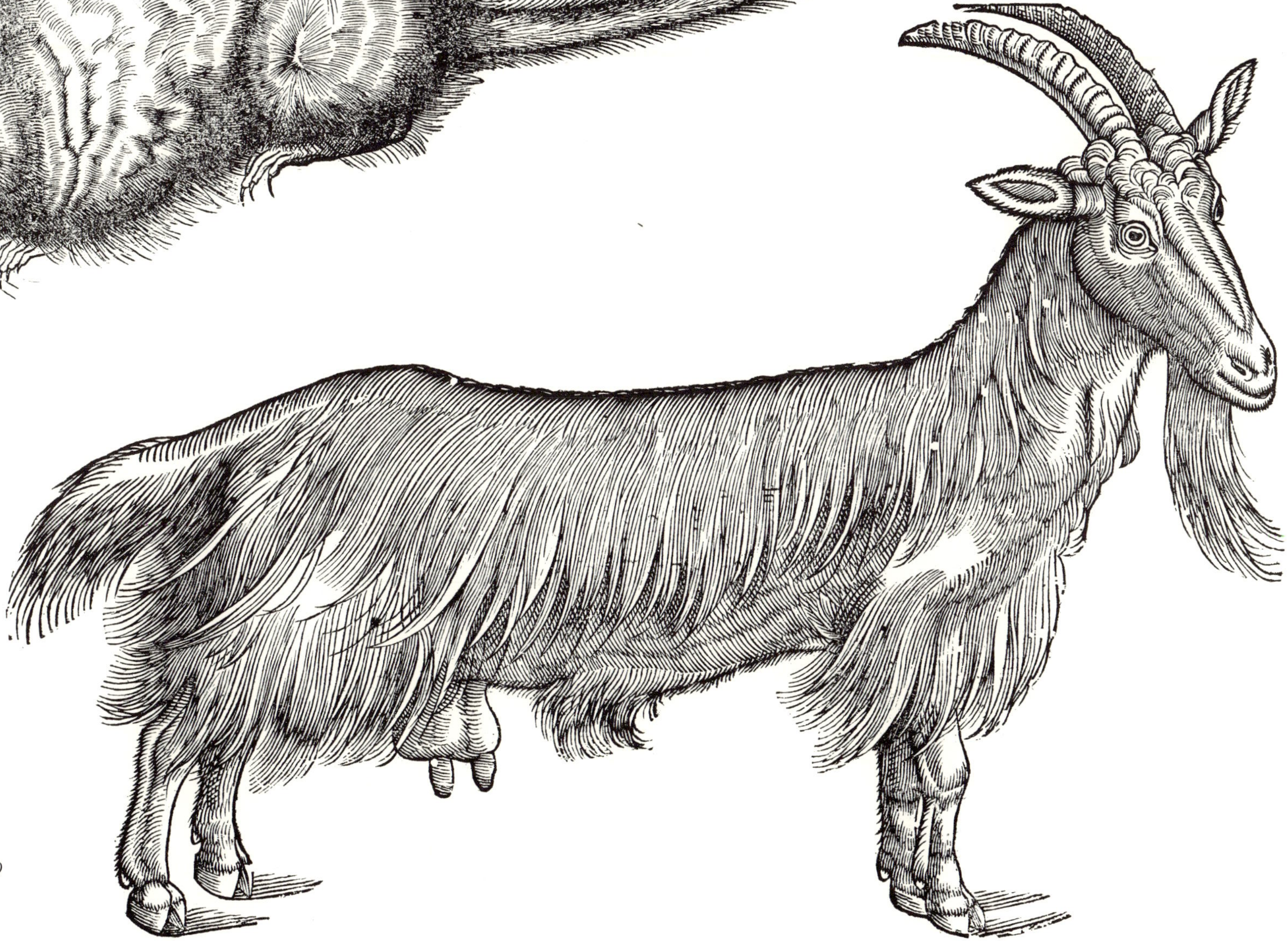

29

28. Rat. 29. Domestic goat (nanny).

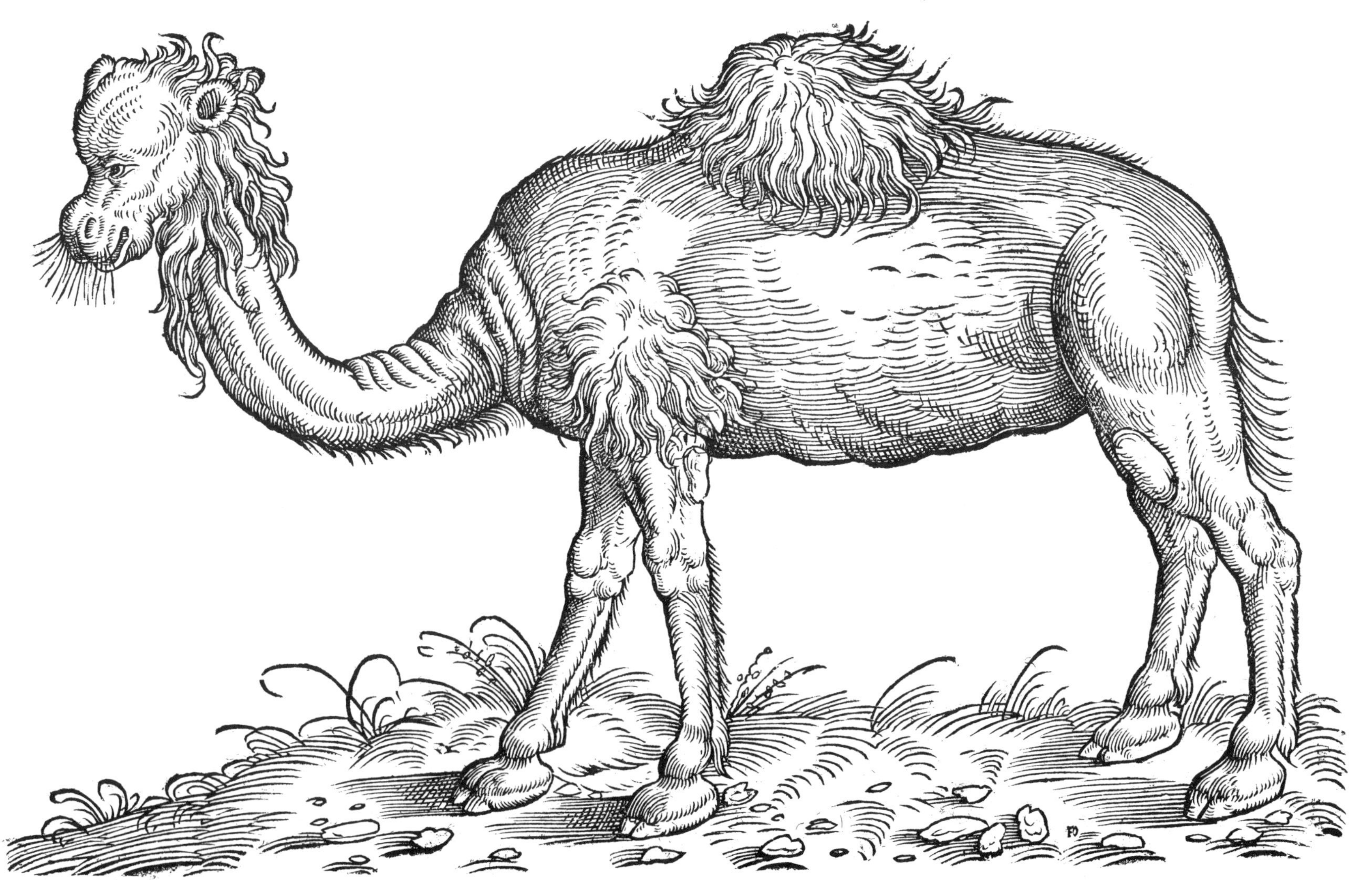

30

30. Dromedary camel.

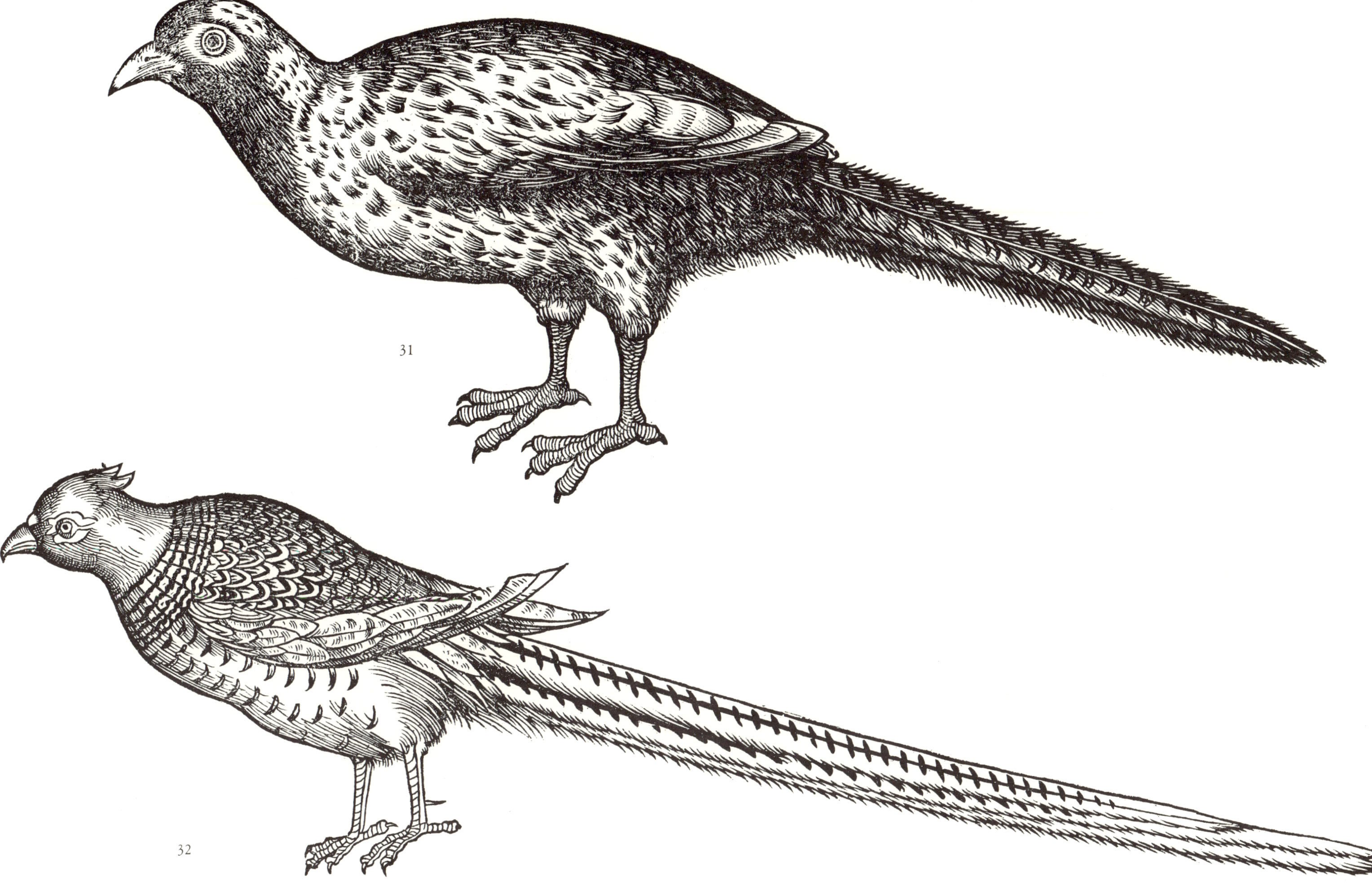

31 and 32. Pheasants.

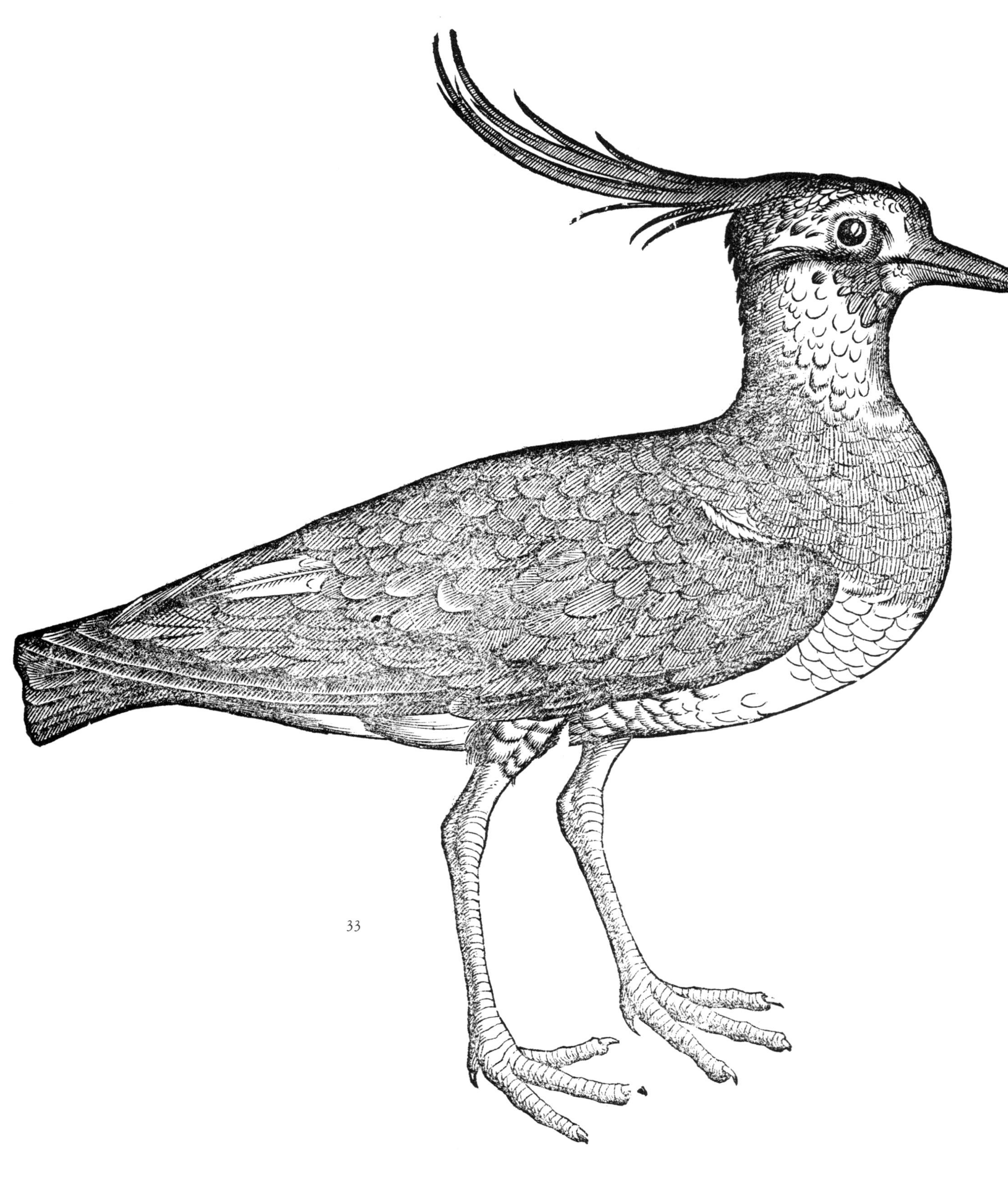

33. Lapwing.

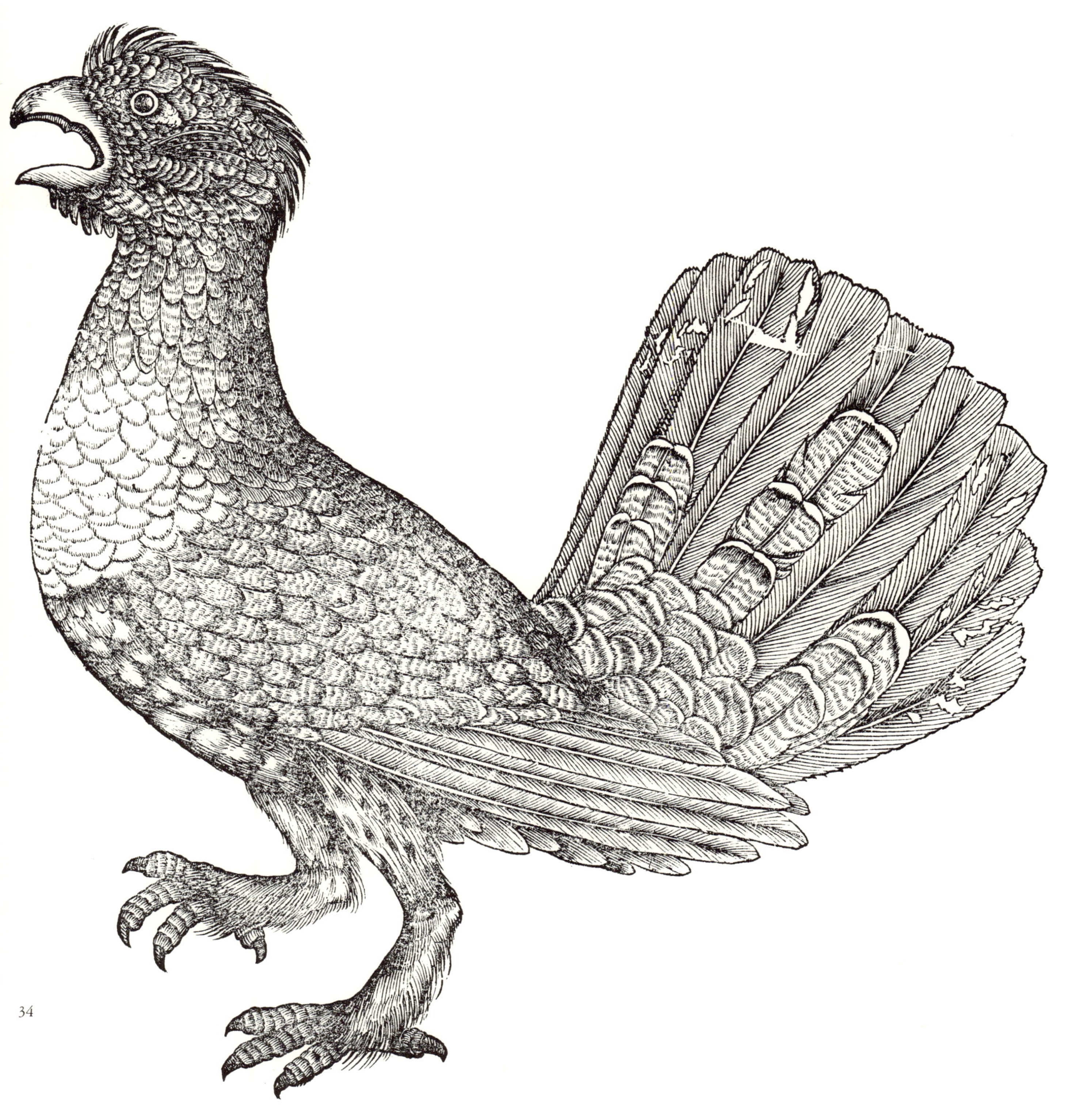

34

34. Heath cock or wood grouse.

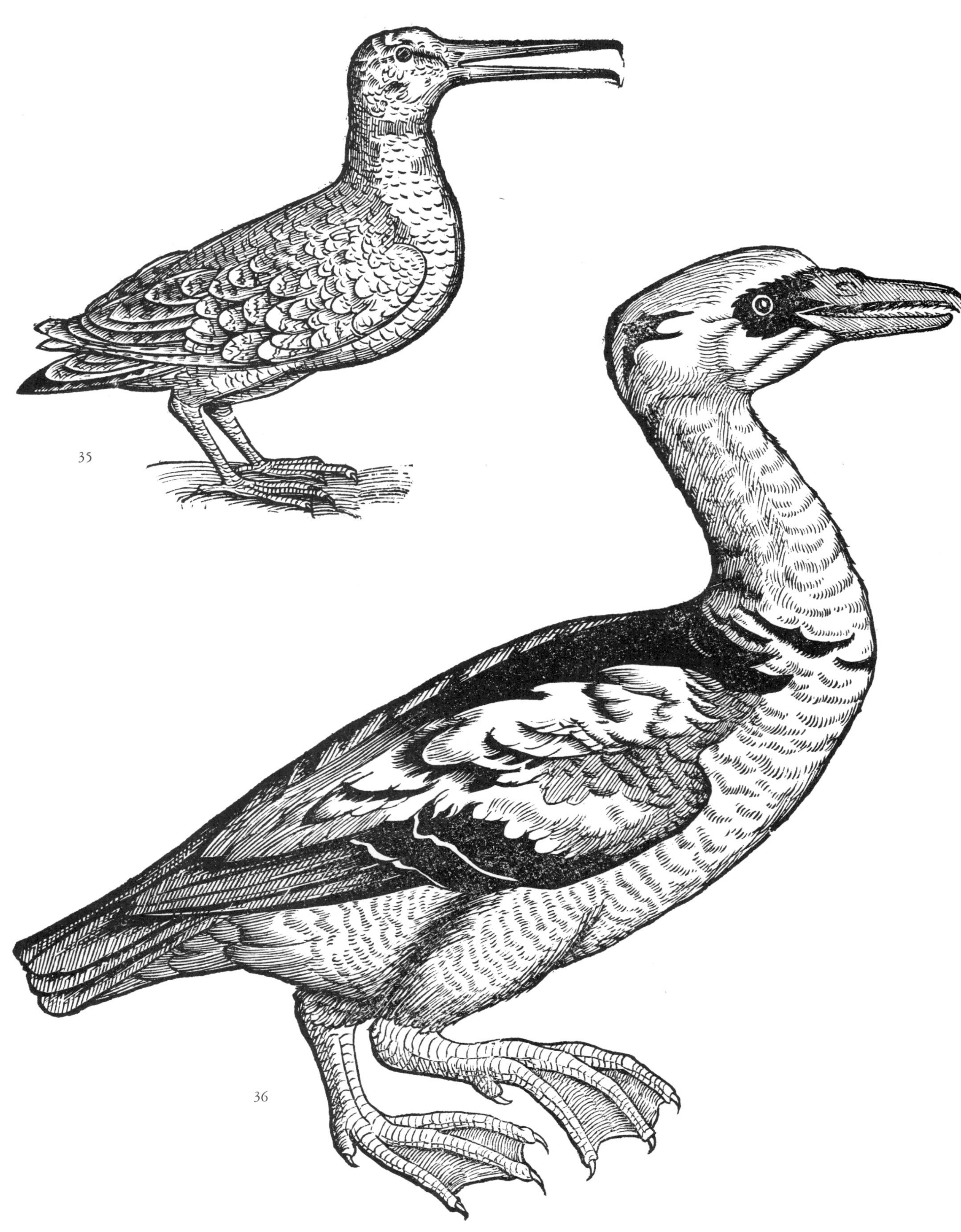

35. Snipe or woodcock. 36. Smew (a fish-eating duck).

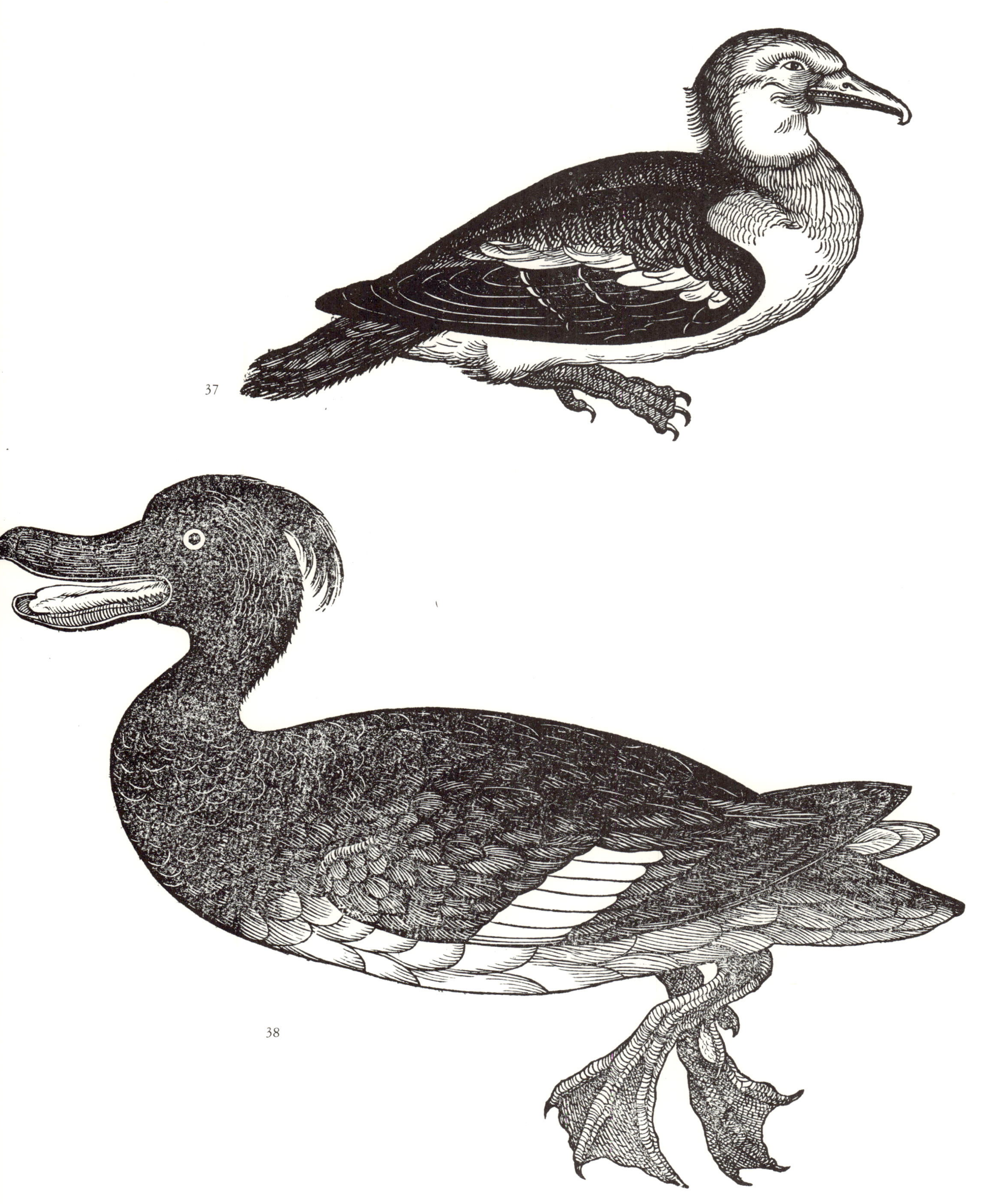

37. Another fish-eating duck, perhaps a type of merganser. 38. Tufted duck.

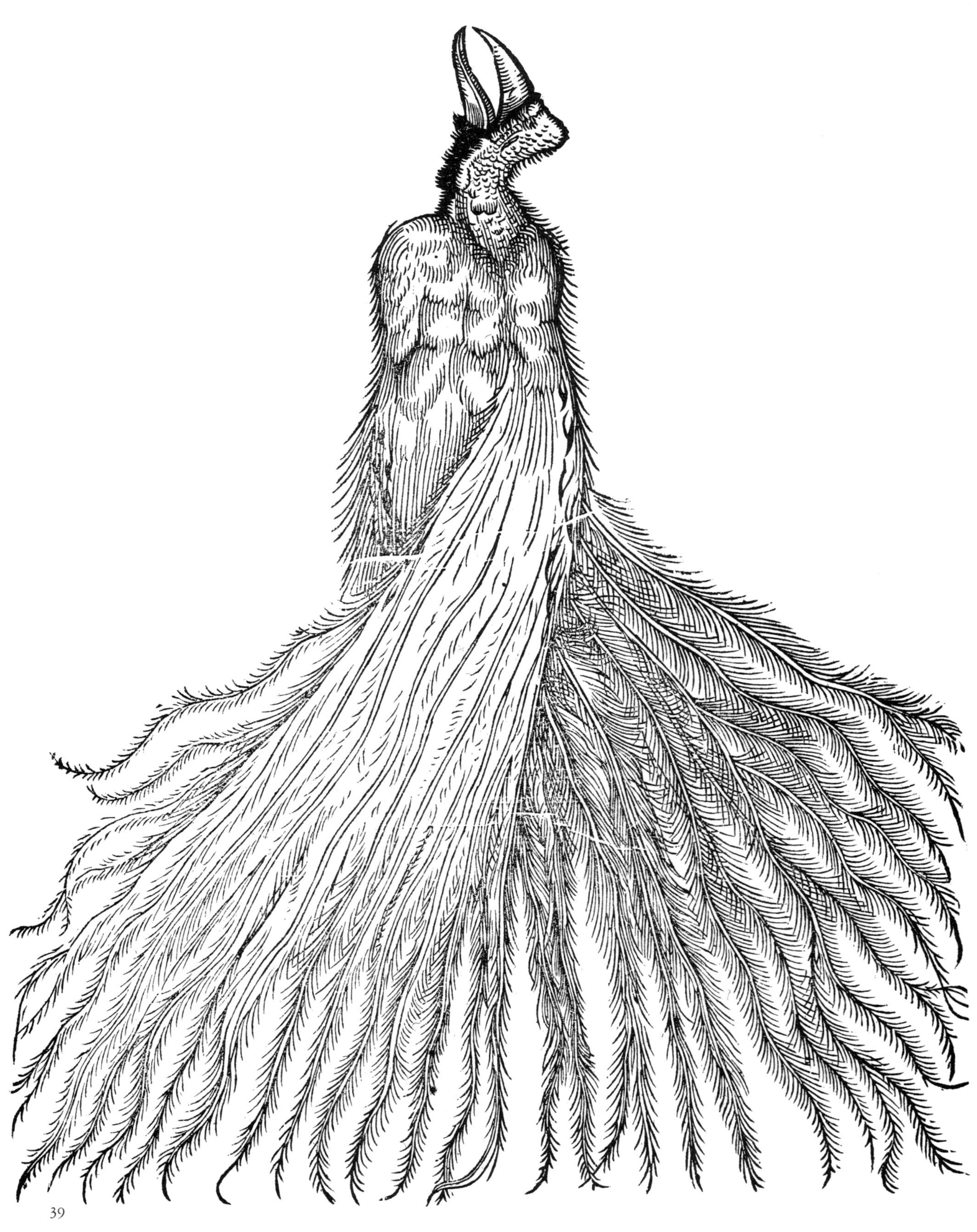
39

39. Bird of paradise.

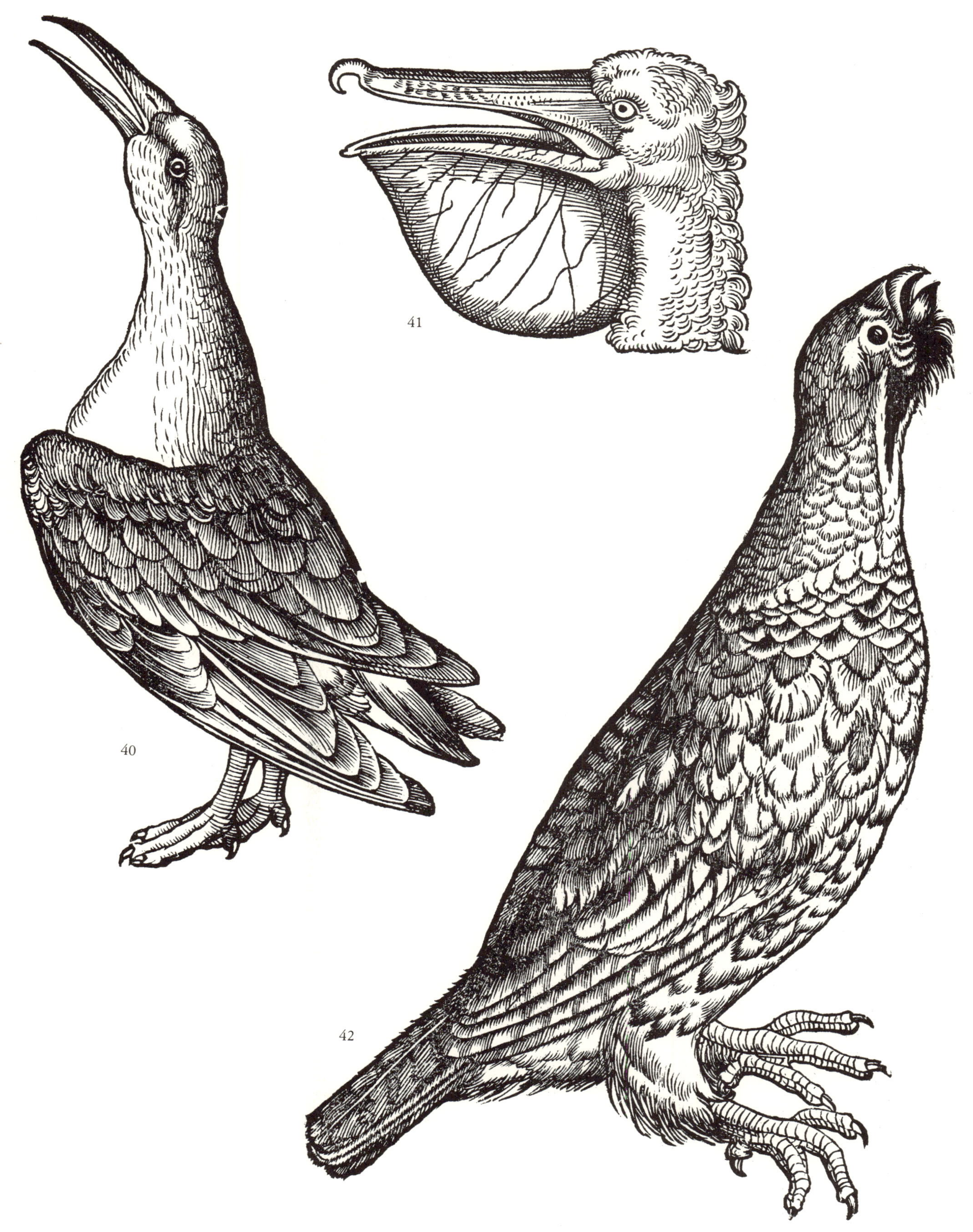

40. A shore bird, perhaps the dunlin (German, *Rotknillis*). 41. Head of pelican. 42. Hazel hen.

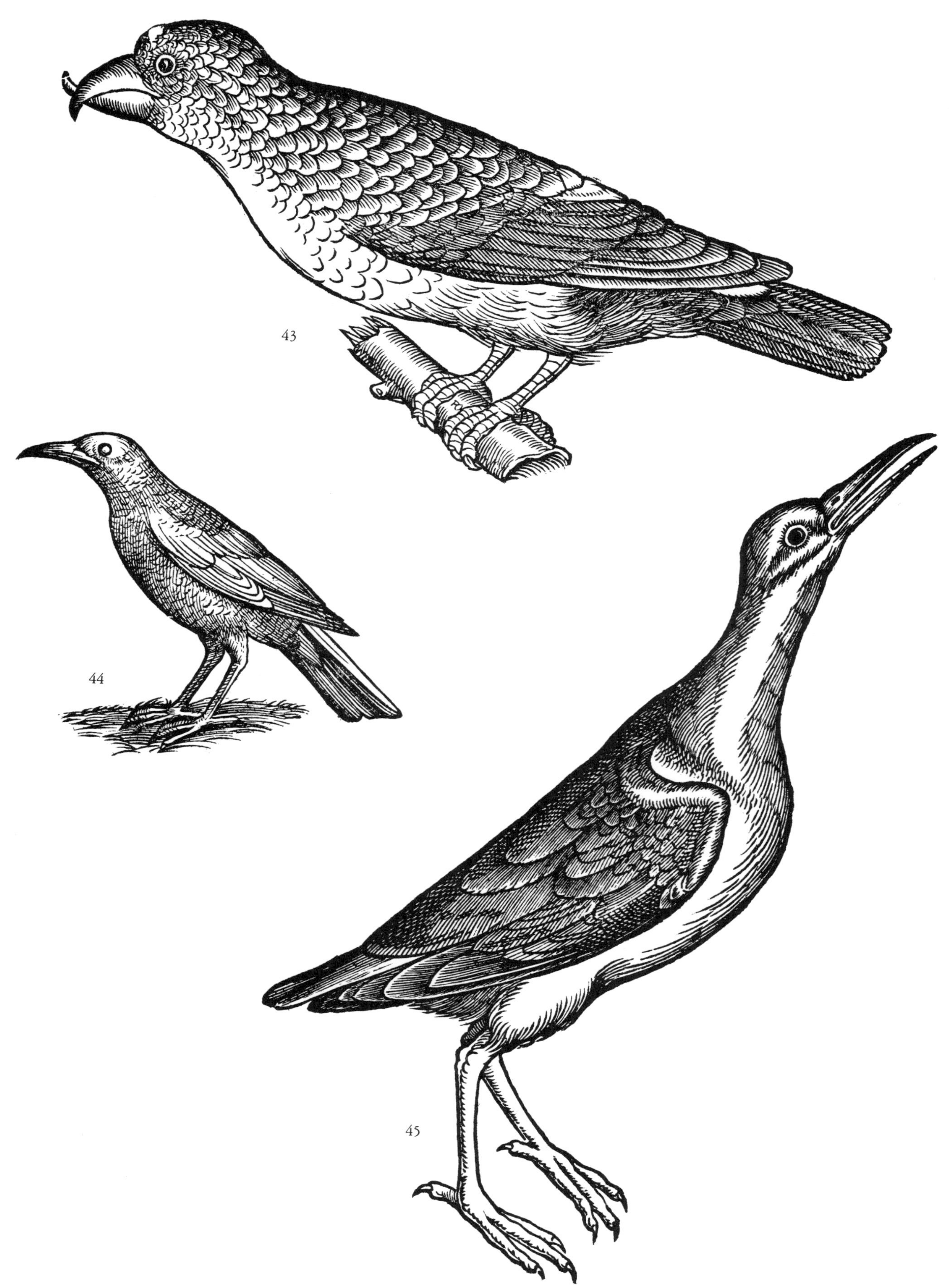

43. Crossbill. 44. Blackbird. 45. A shore bird, perhaps the redshank (German, *Fysterin*).

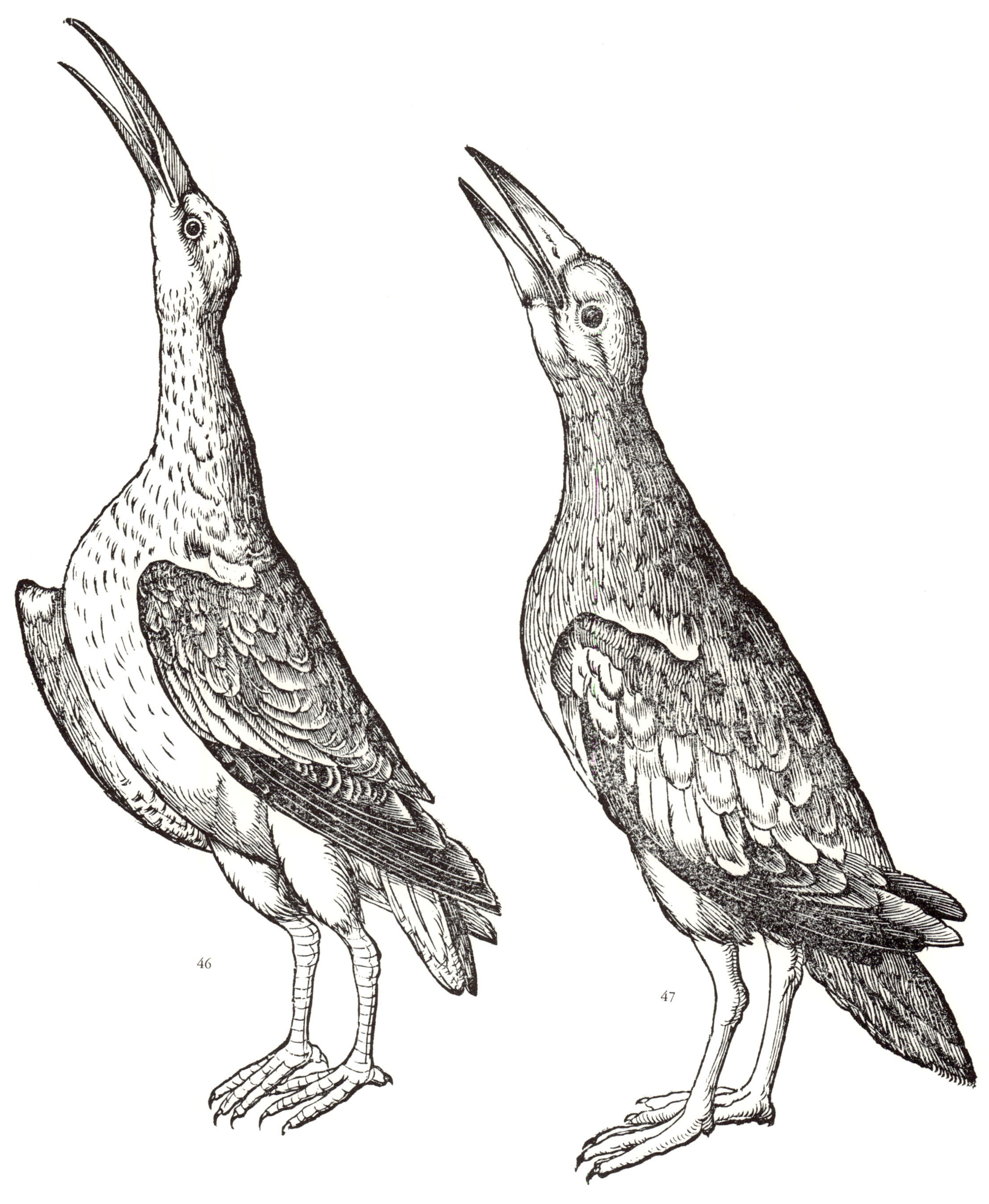

46. Whimbrel. 47. Green sandpiper.

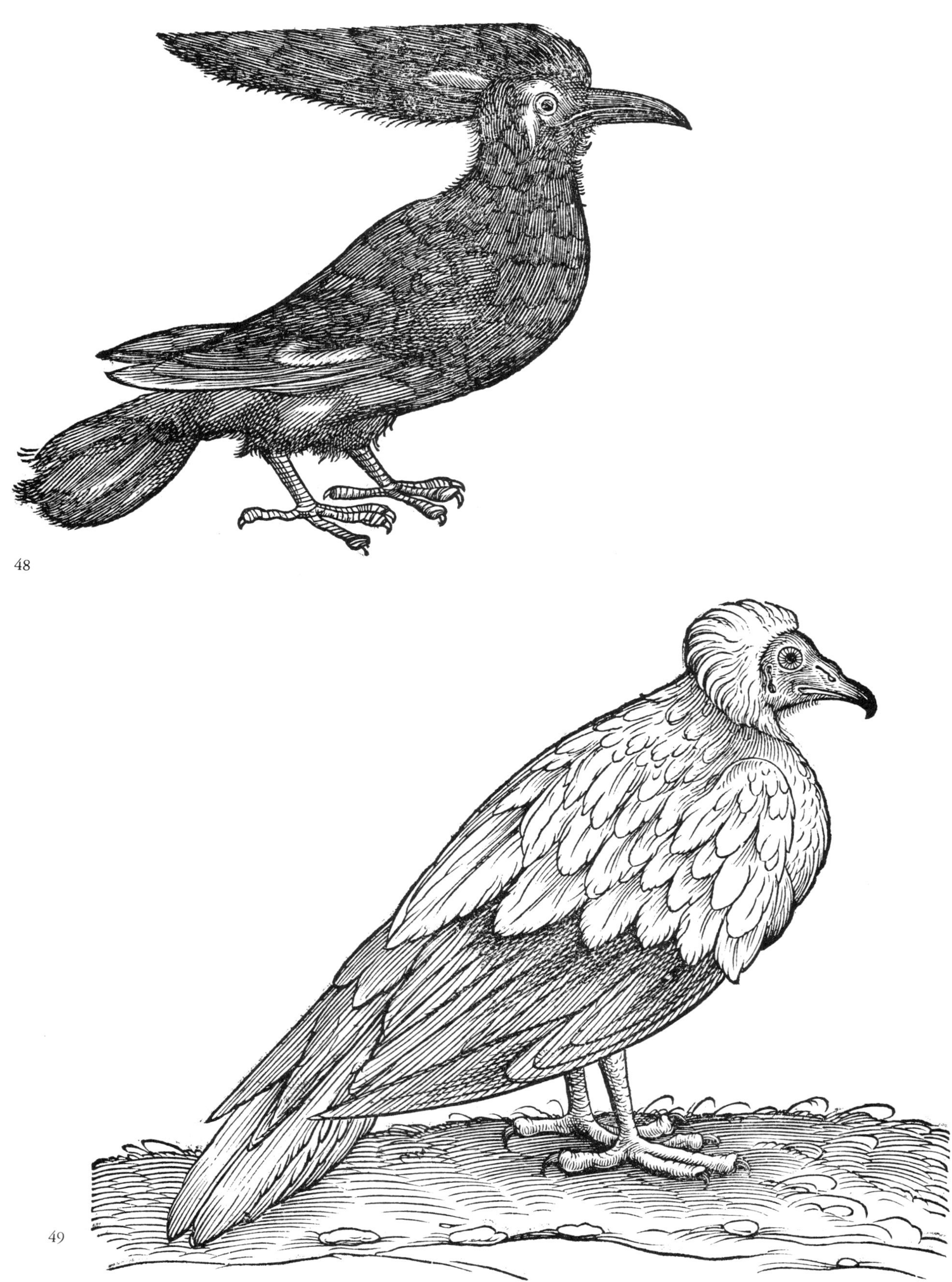

48

49

48. An unidentified South American bird. 49. Egyptian vulture.

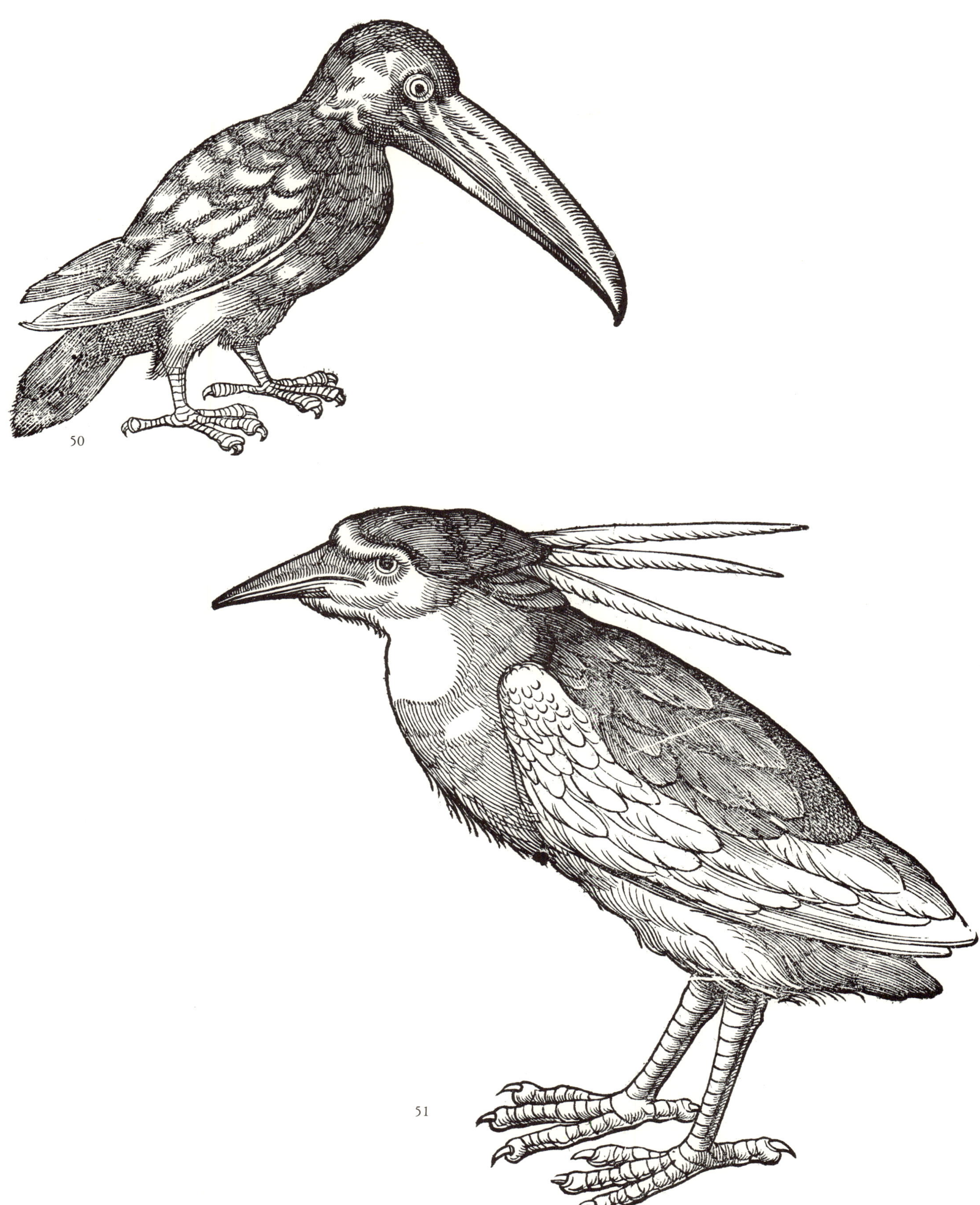

50. Toucan. 51. Night heron.

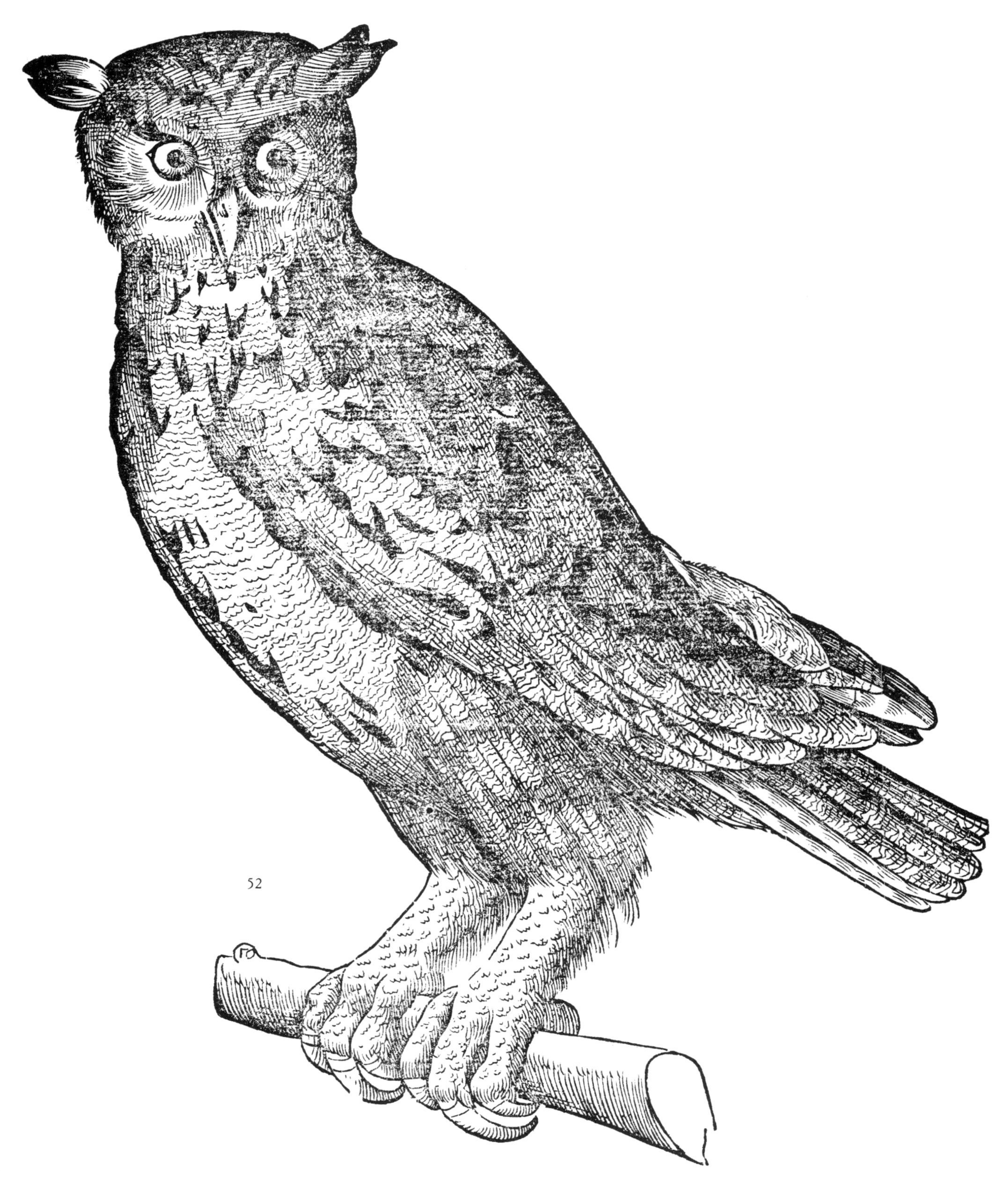

52. Eagle owl, the largest European owl.

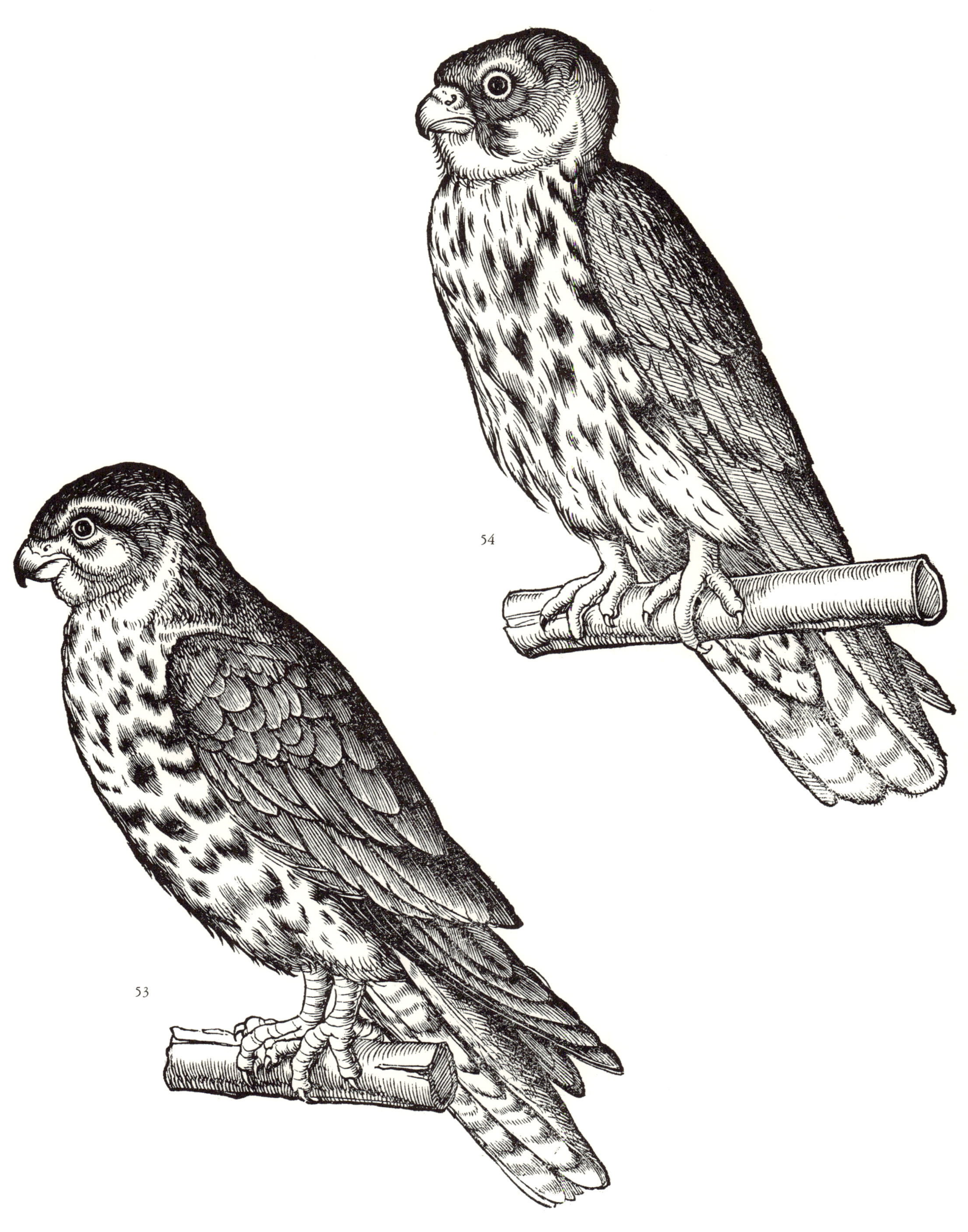

53. Merlin (a type of falcon). 54. Hobby (another type of falcon).

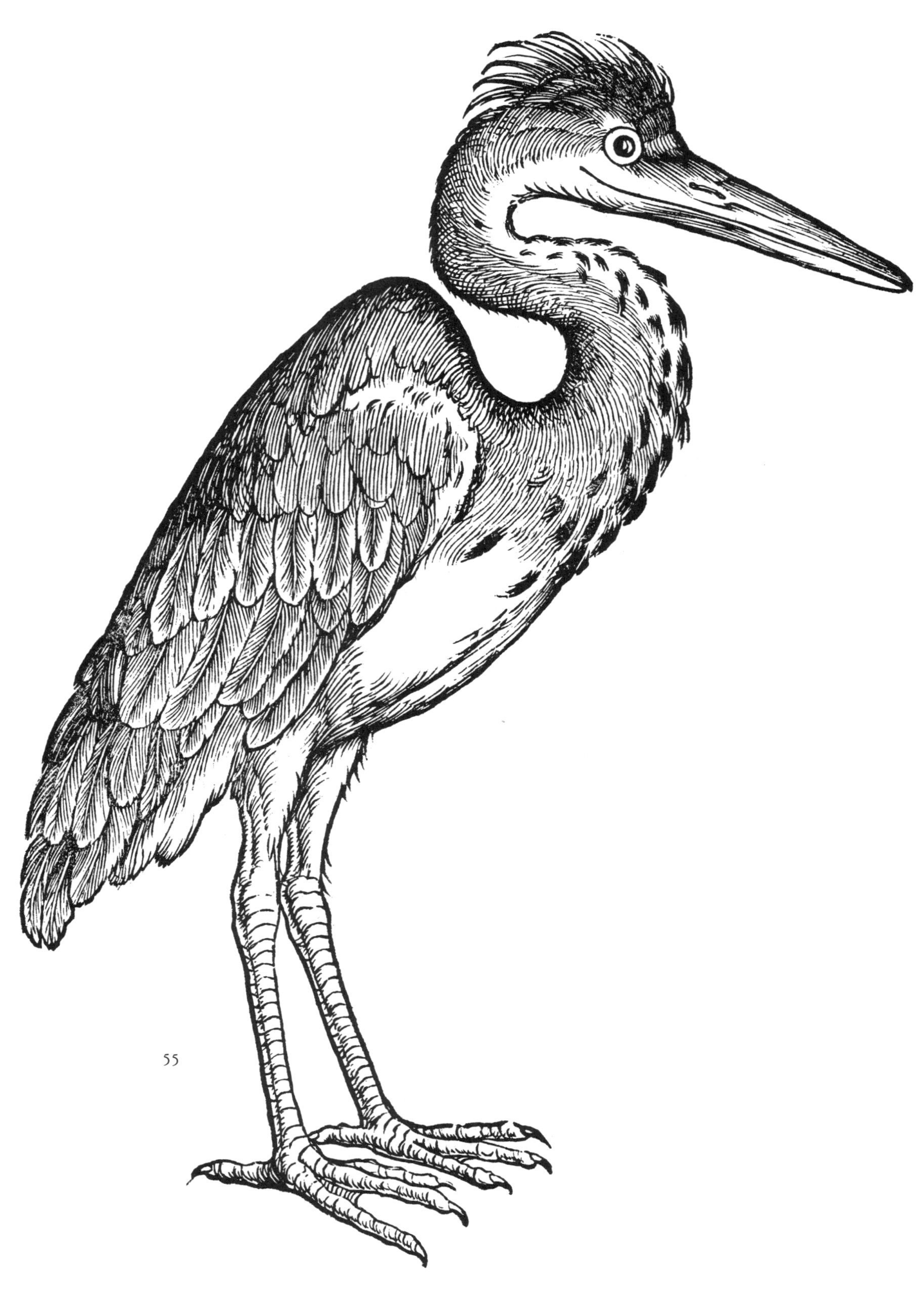

55. A heron, probably the blue.

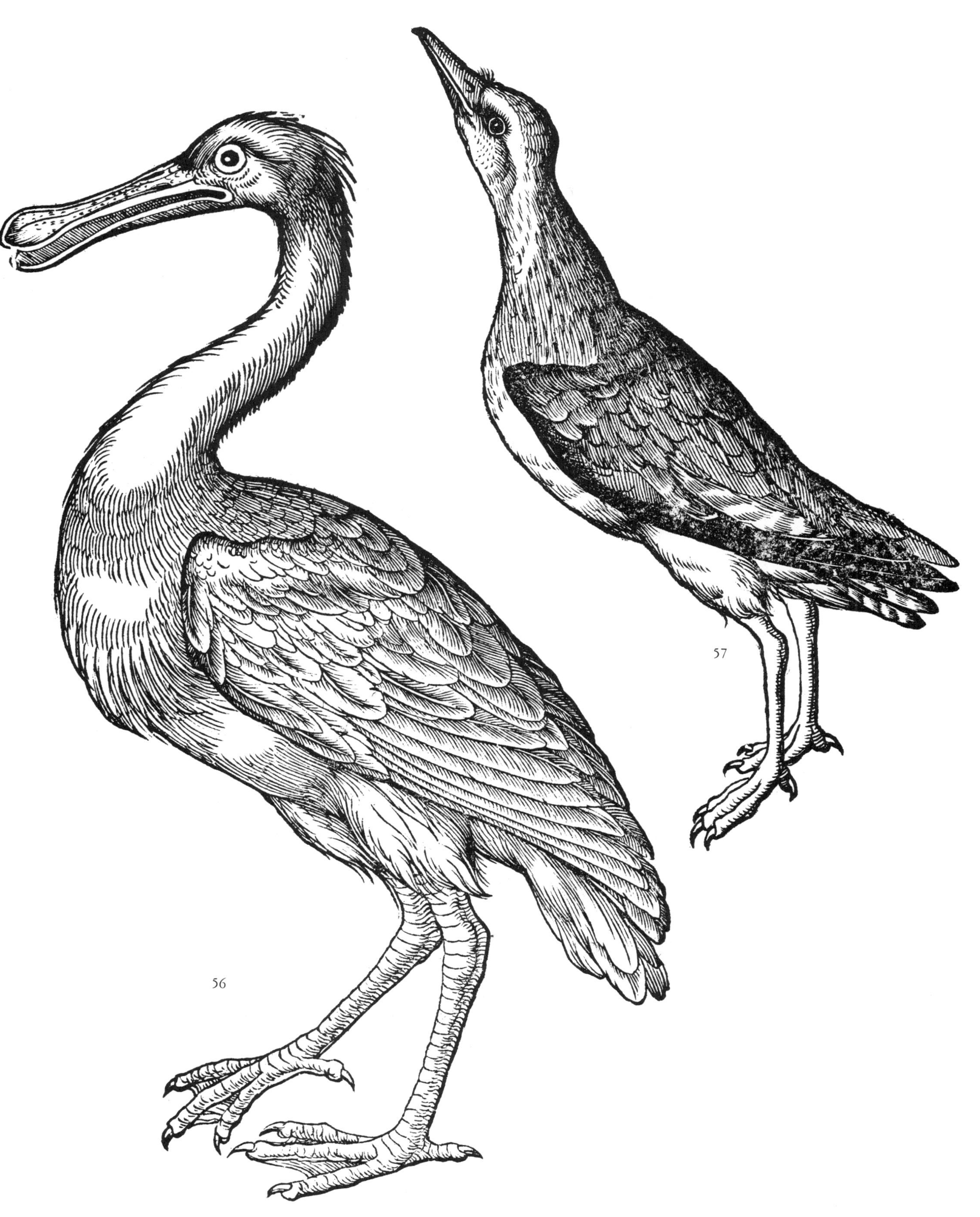

56. Spoonbill. 57. A shore bird, perhaps the greenshank (German, *Mattknillis*).

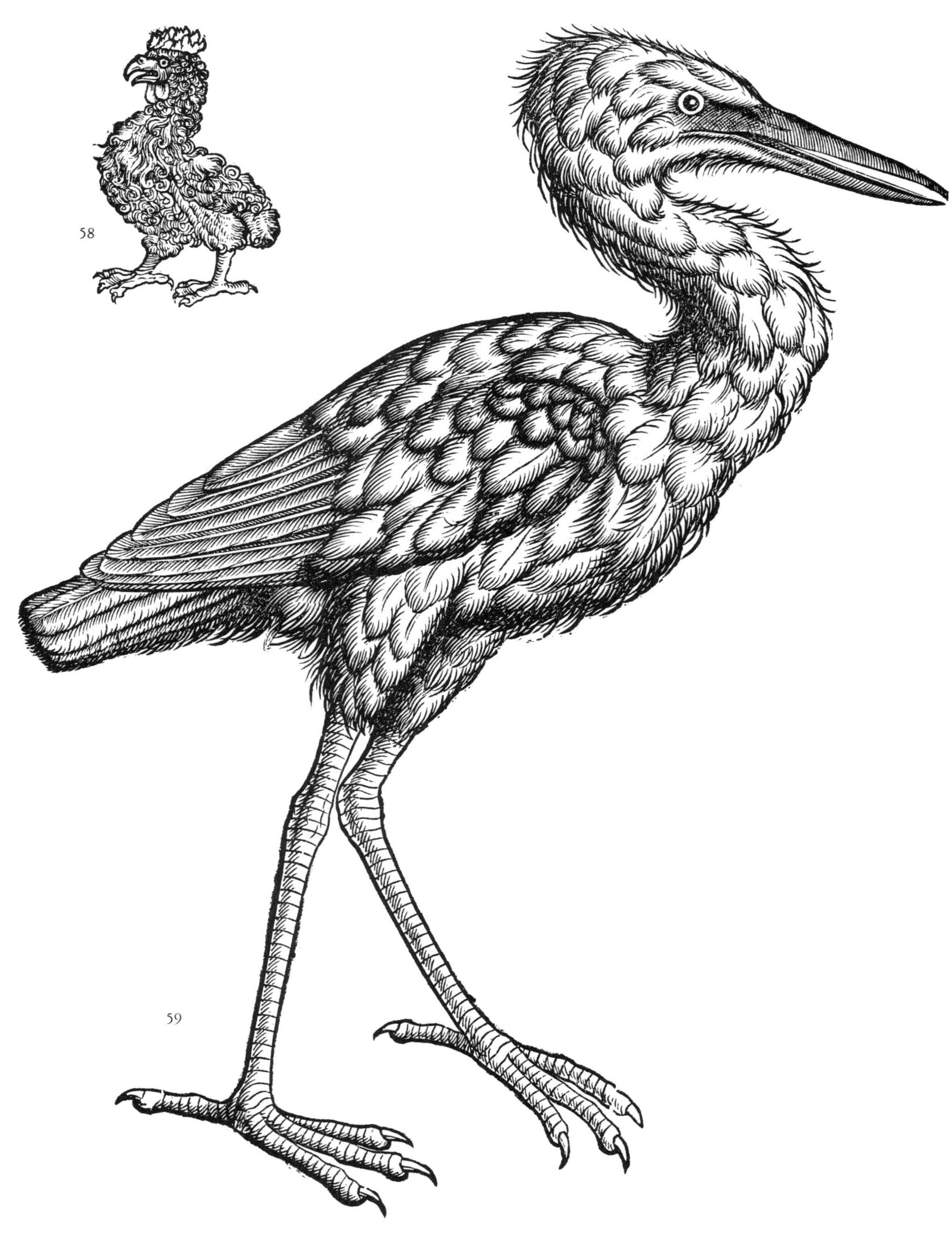

58. A woolly chicken. 59. Great white heron.

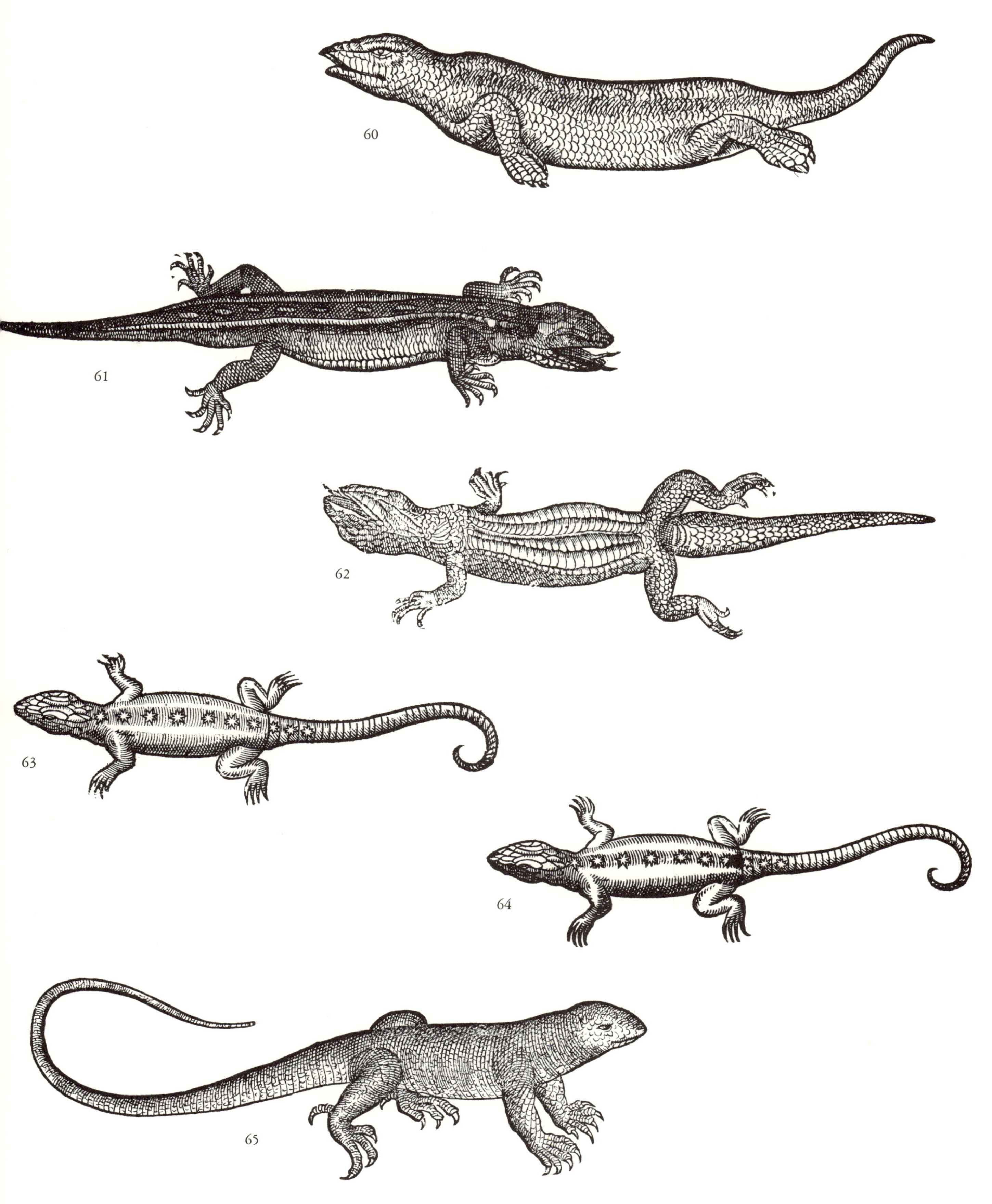

60. Skink. 61. A type of lizard. 62. A type of lizard (shown belly up). 63 and 64. Stellions (a type of lizard). 65. A Brazilian land lizard.

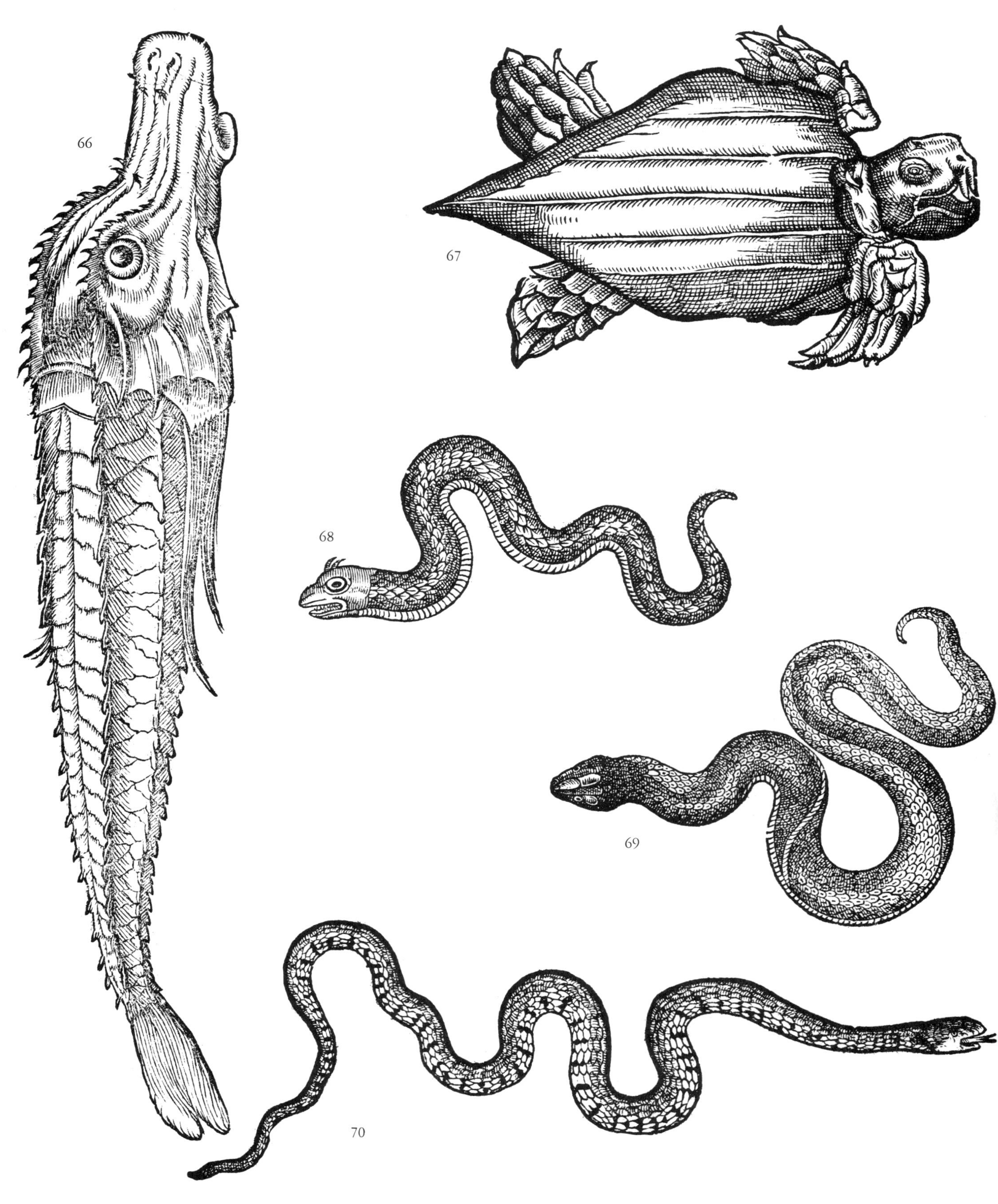

66. "Lamprey." 67. Leatherback turtle. 68. "Horned serpent" or cerastes.
69. "Millet" or "cenchrine" (a type of snake). 70. "Water adder."

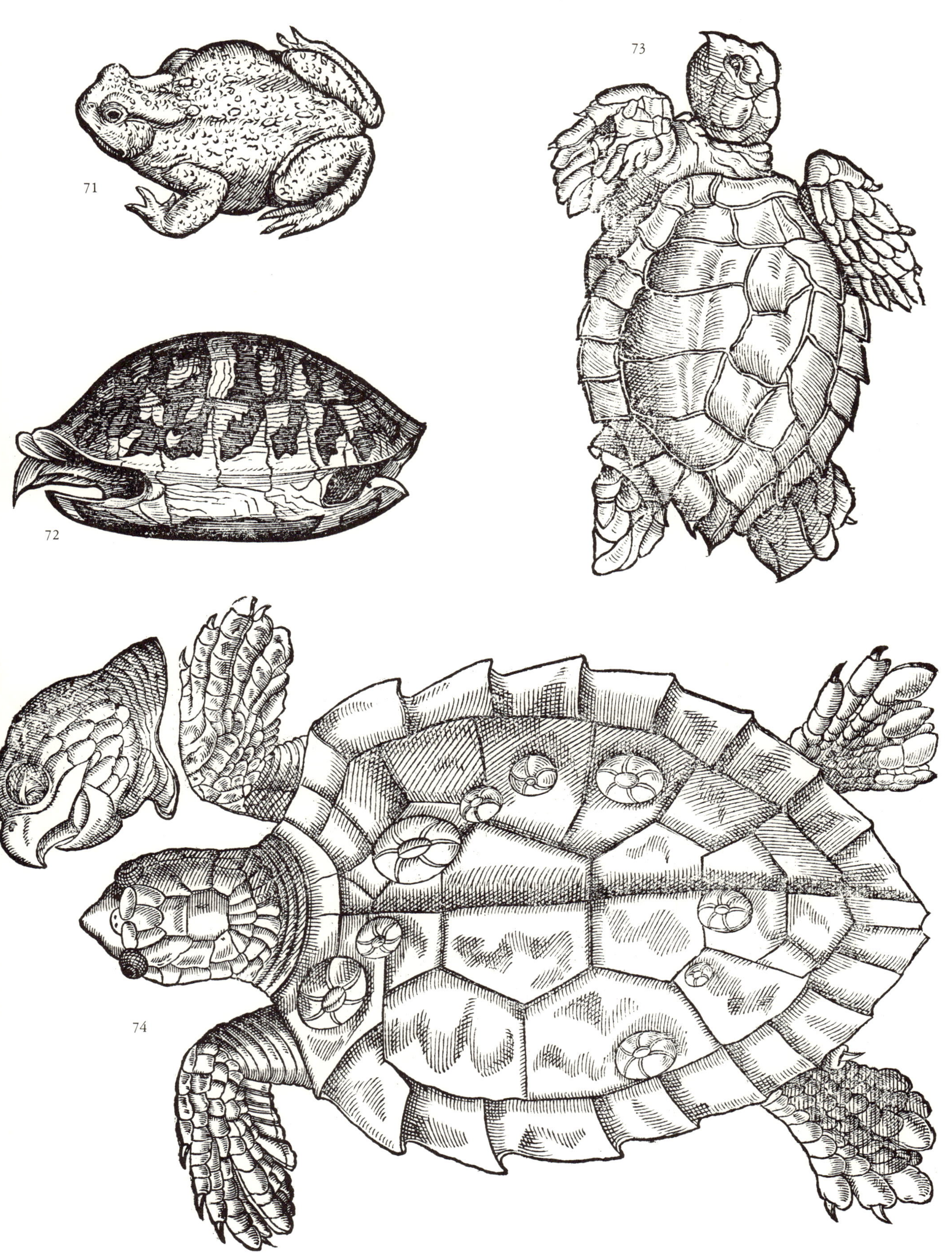

71. Toad. 72. Land tortoise. 73 and 74. Marine turtles.

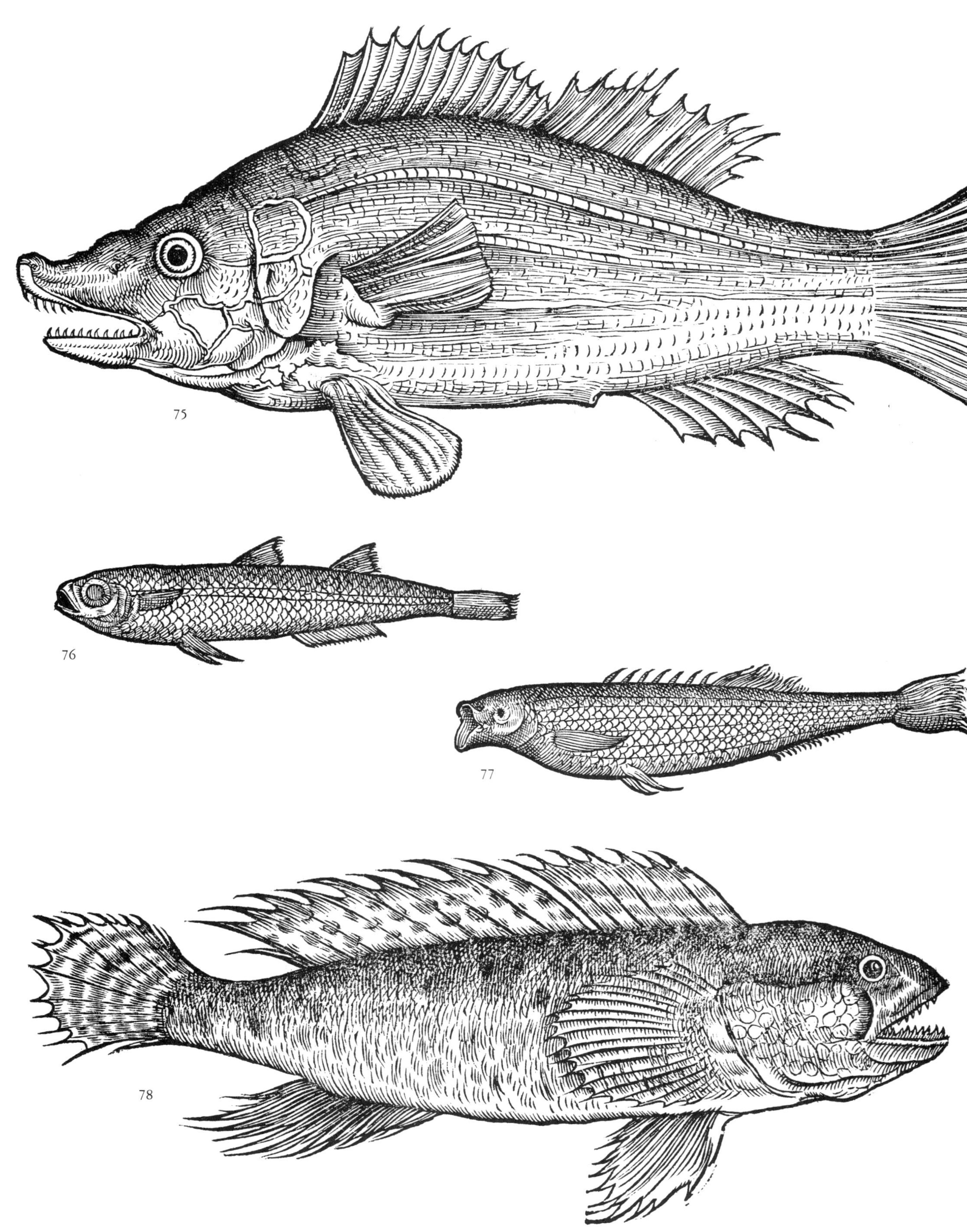

75. A type of wrasse. 76. Silversides or sand smelt. 77. A type of stickleback. 78. A type of goby.

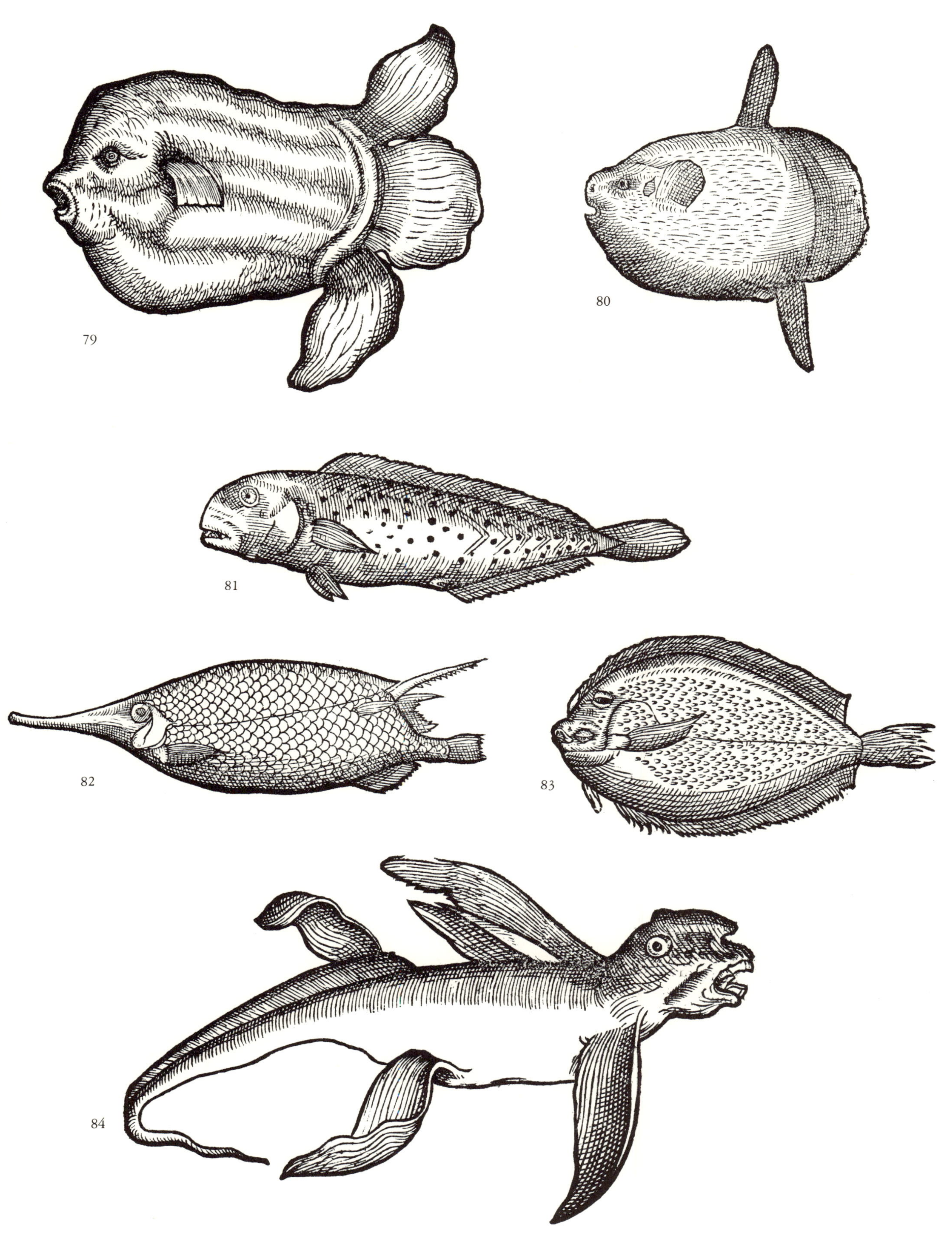

79 and 80. Sunfish. 81. Shanny or blenny. 82. Snipe fish or trumpet-fish. 83. A type of flatfish. 84. Elephant fish or chimaera.

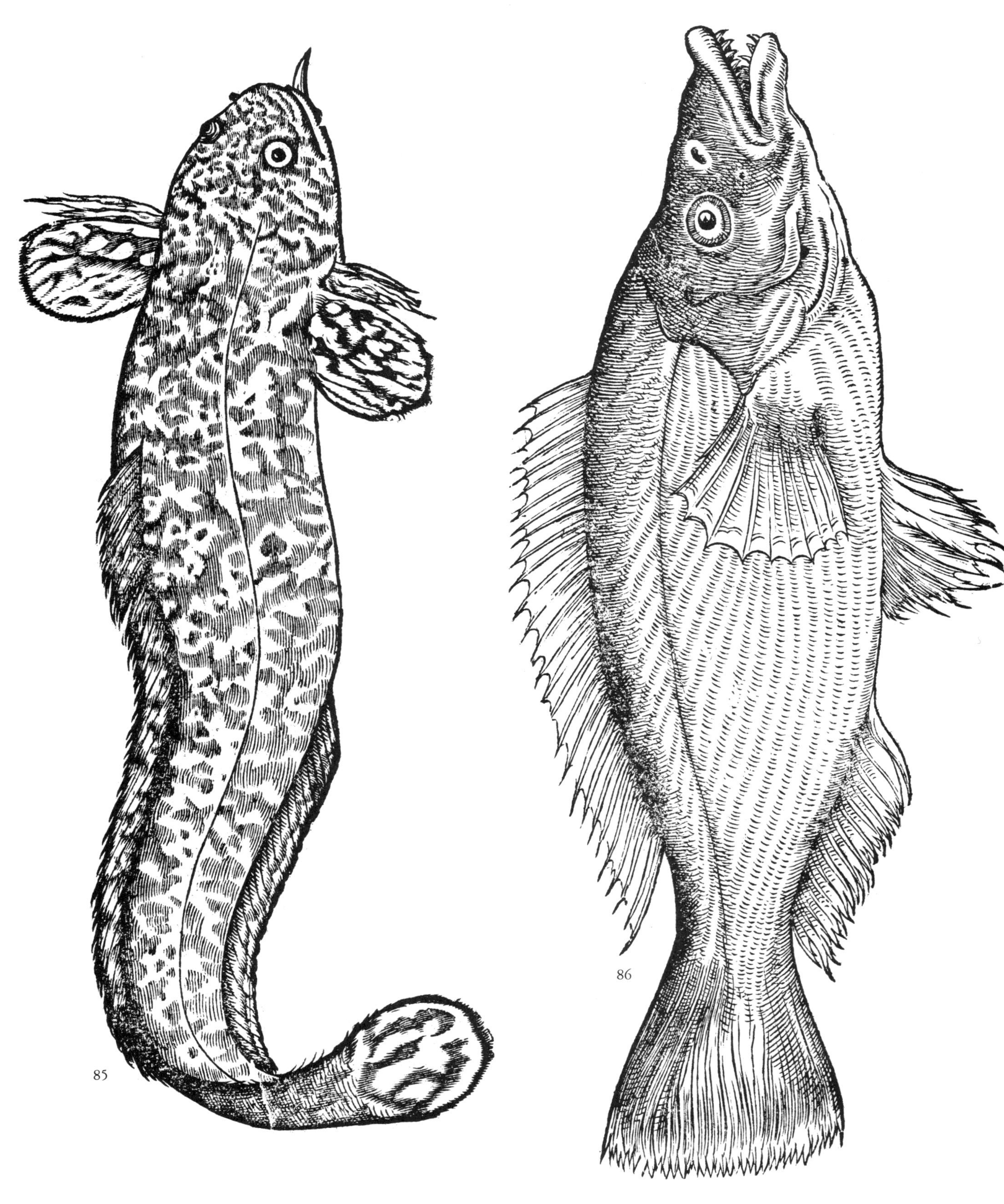

85. Burbot. 86. A type of wrasse, perhaps the rainbow wrasse.

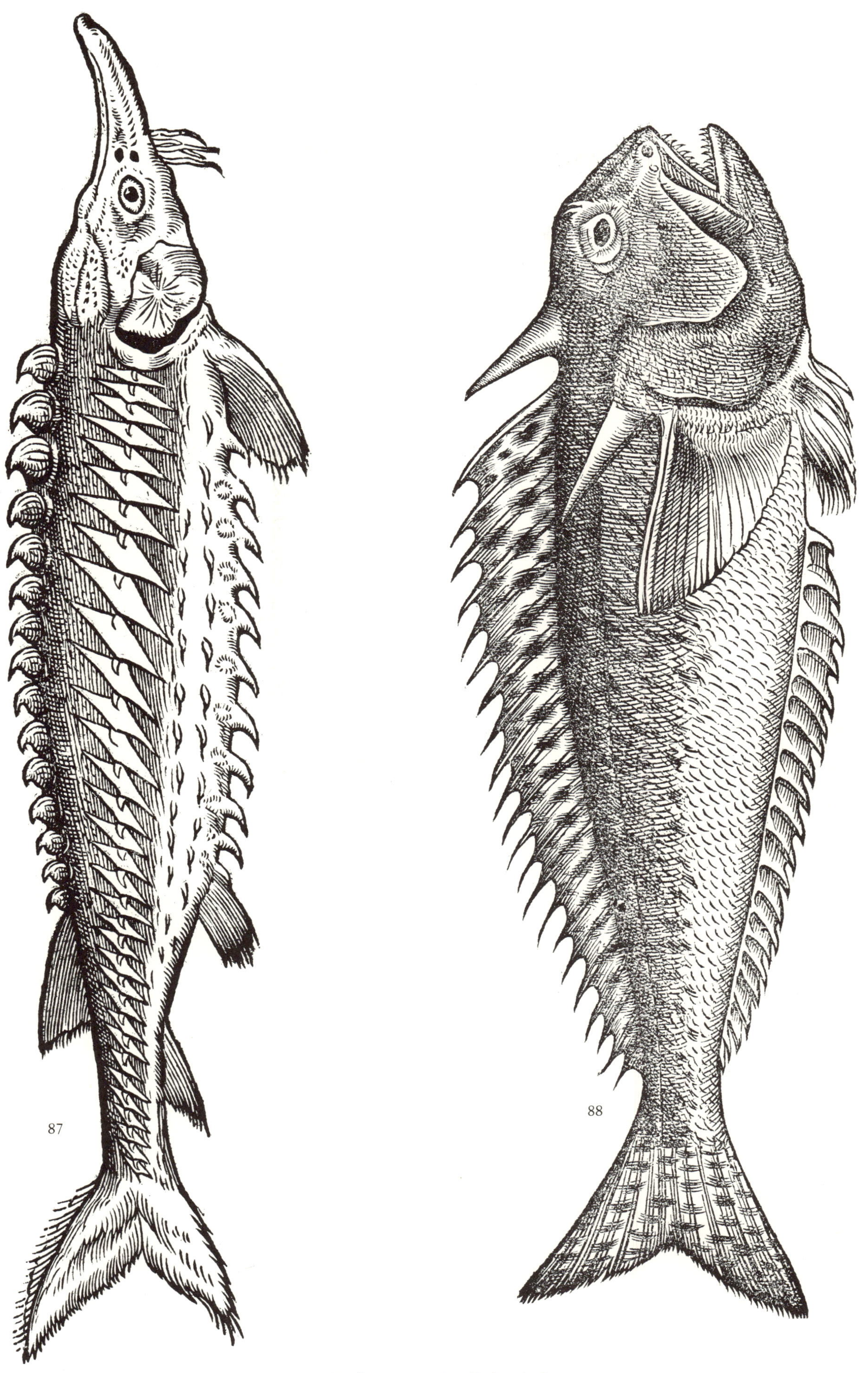

87. Sturgeon. 88. Father-lasher.

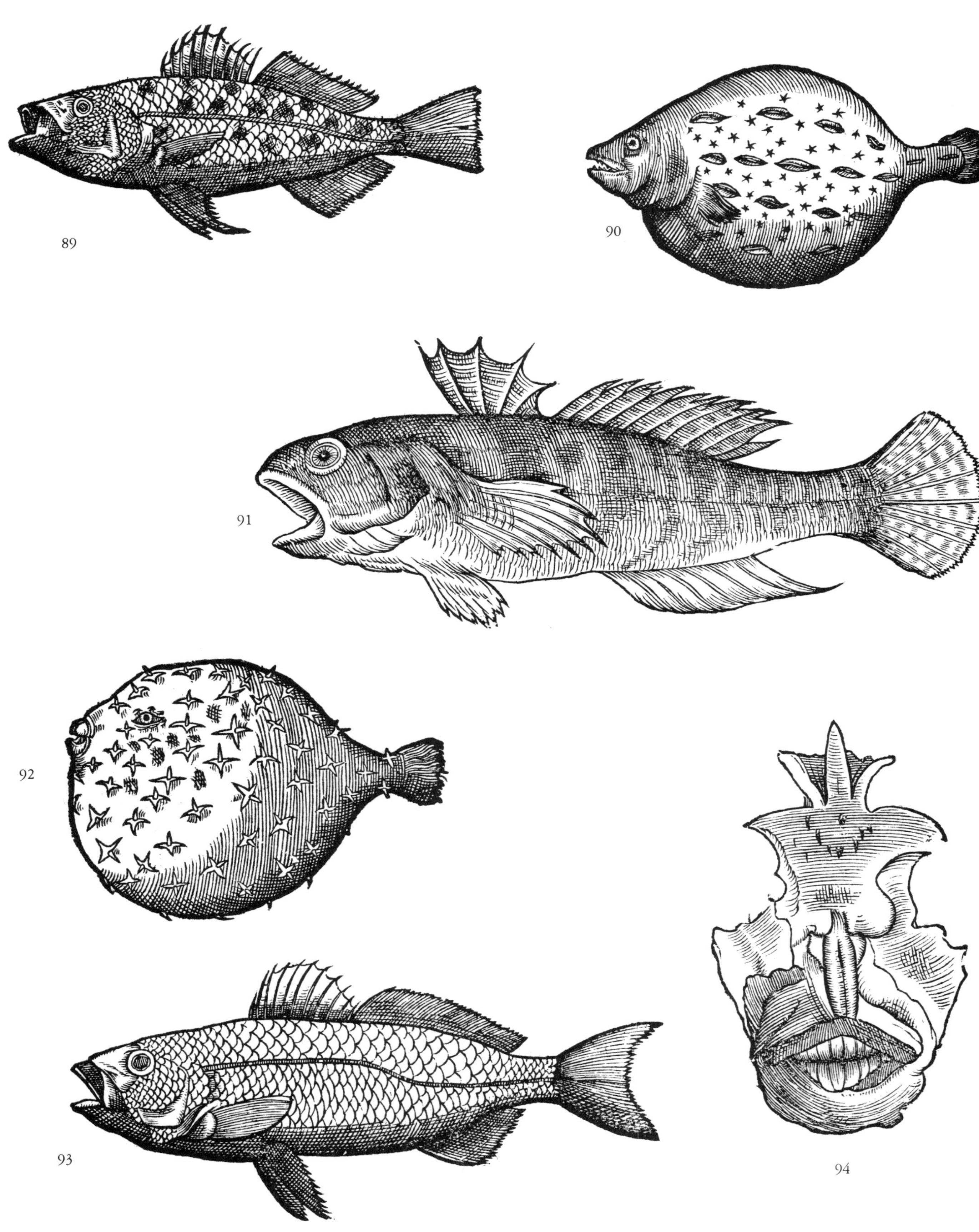

89 and 93. Sea perch or dace (French, *loup*). 90 and 92. Lumpfish. 91. A type of goby.
94. Head of sargo (kin of the American sheepshead).

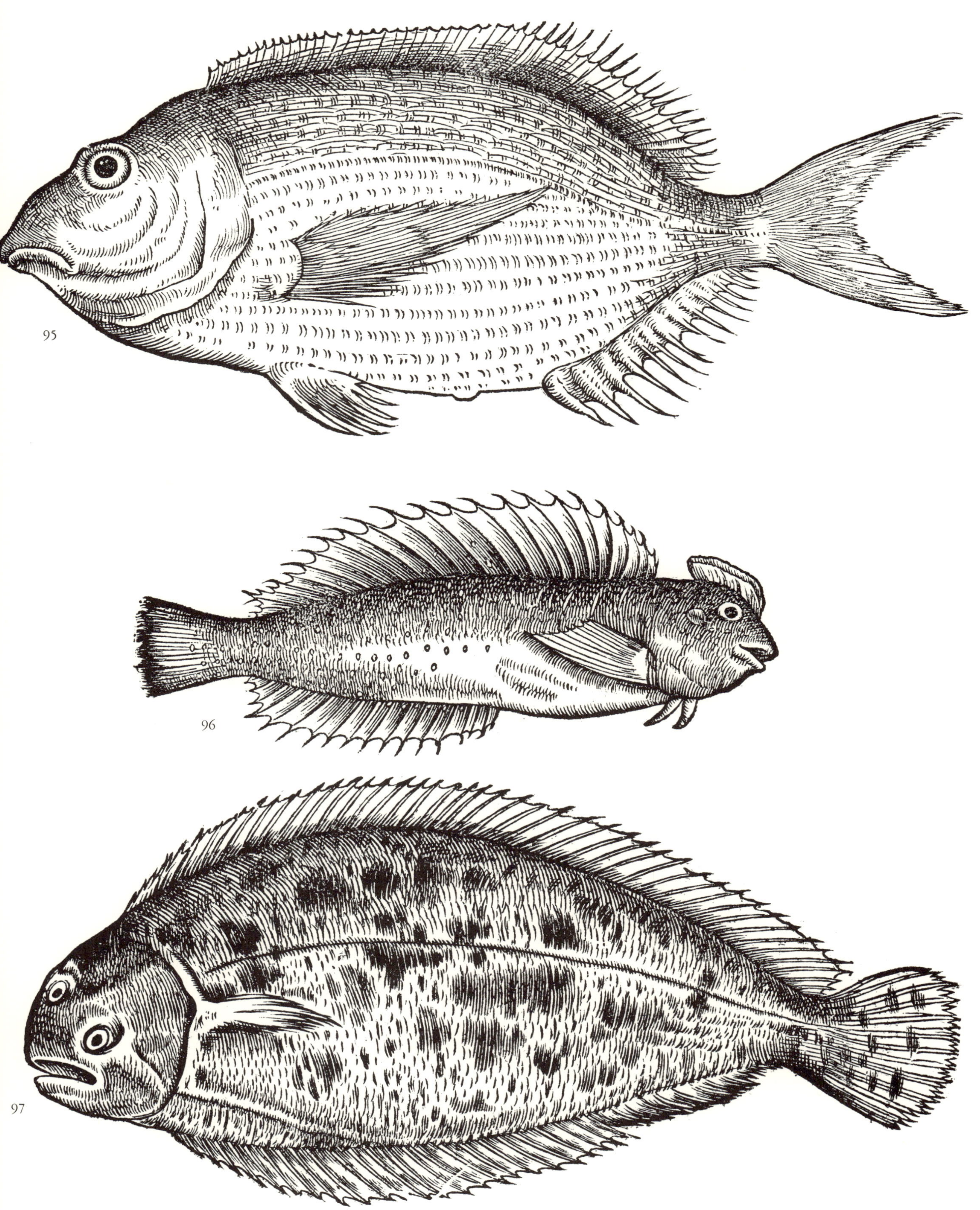

95. Sargo. 96. A type of blenny. 97. Sole.

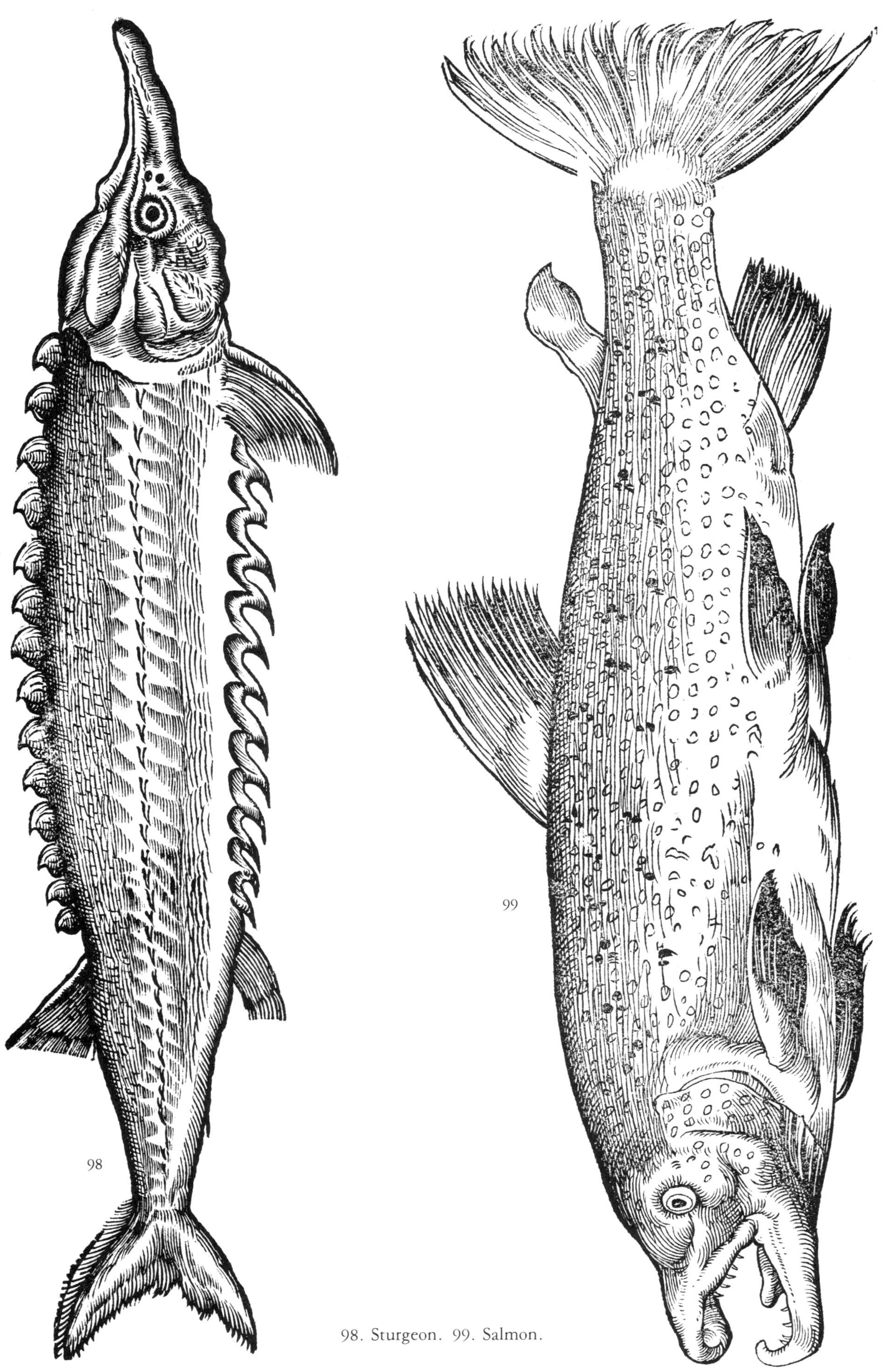

98. Sturgeon. 99. Salmon.

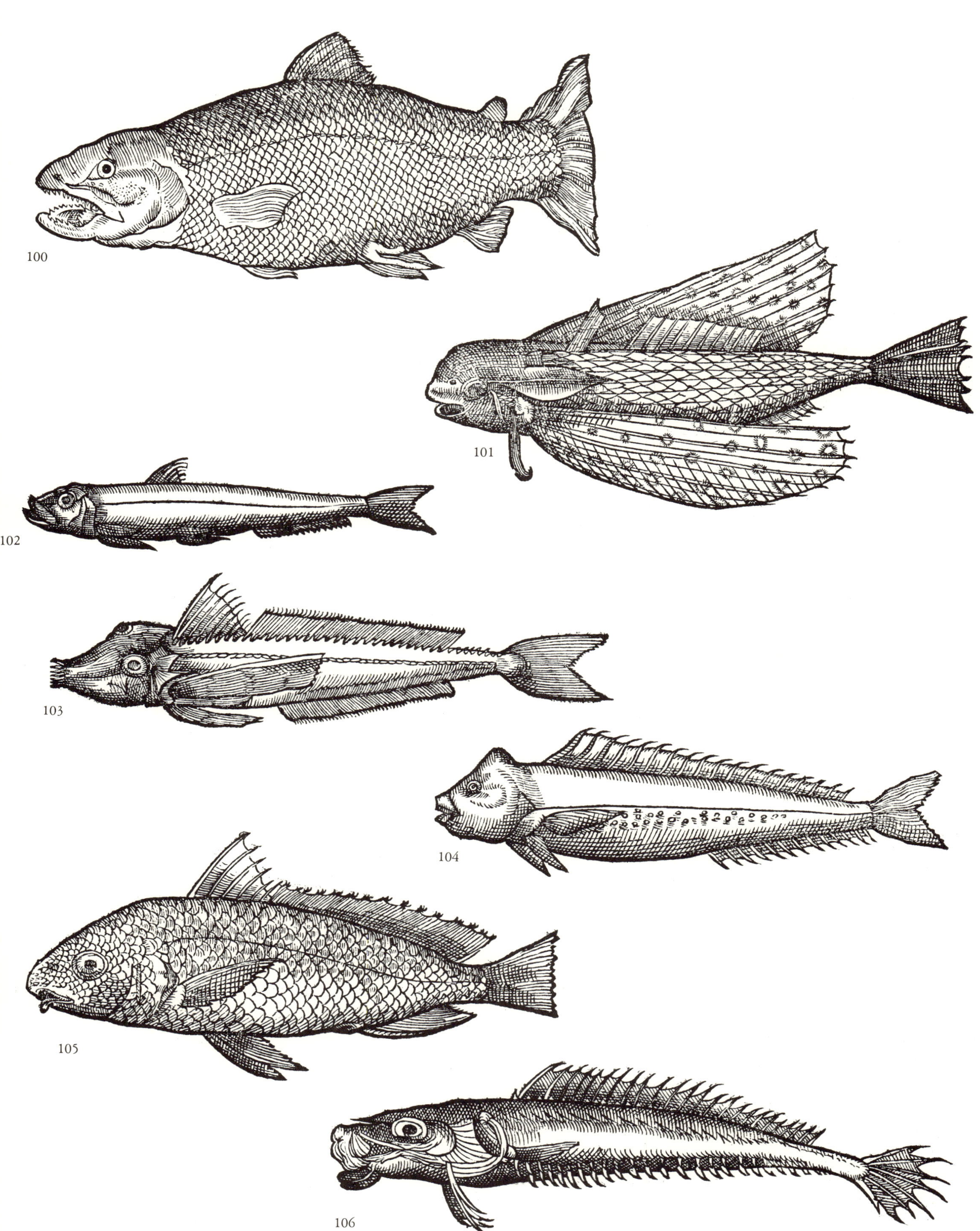

100. Northern char. 101 and 103. Types of gurnard or sea robin. 102. A type of goby. 104. A type of blenny. 105. Umbra. 106. An unidentified fish (*taenia*).

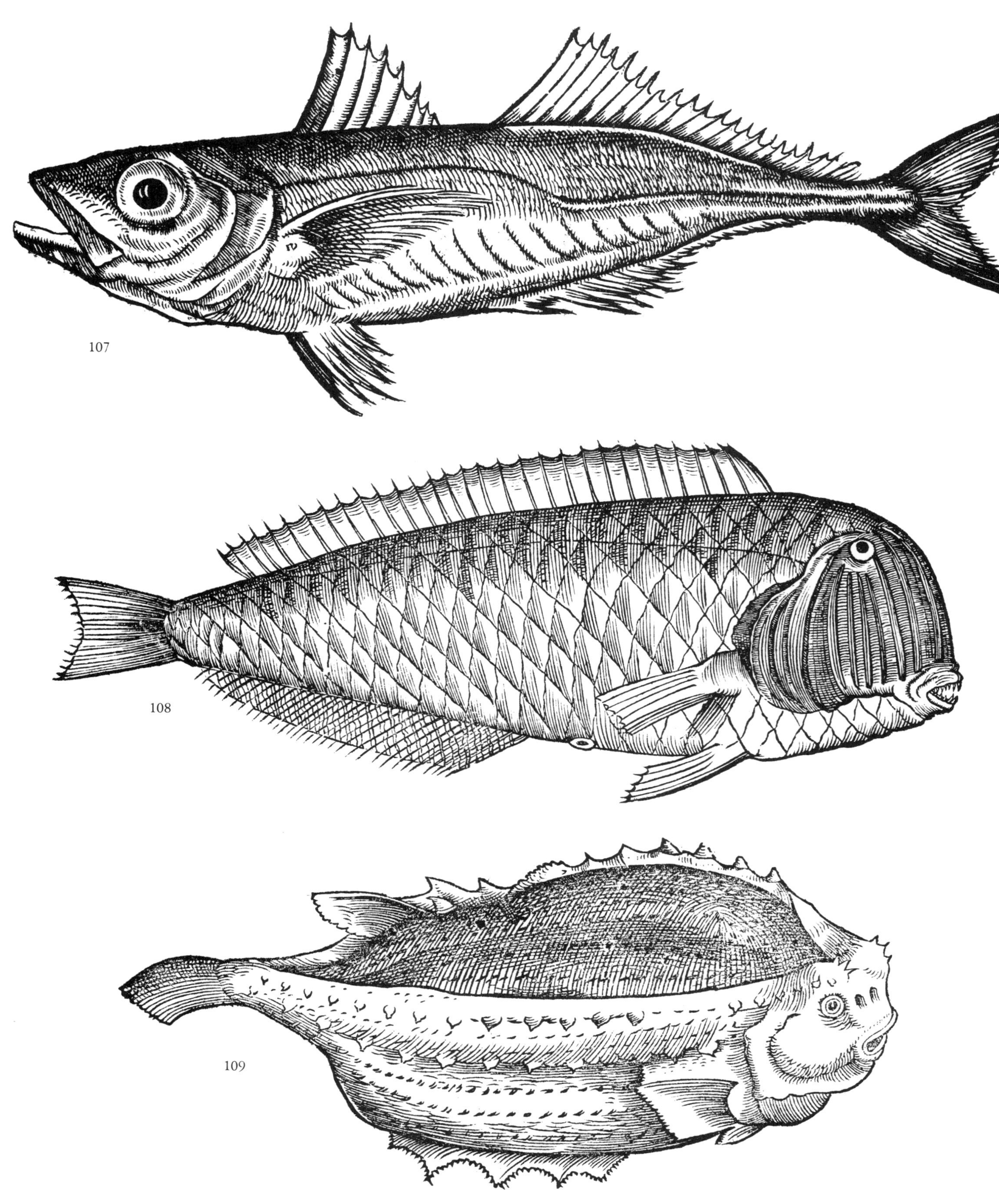

107. Spanish mackerel. 108. Razor fish. 109. Lumpsucker.

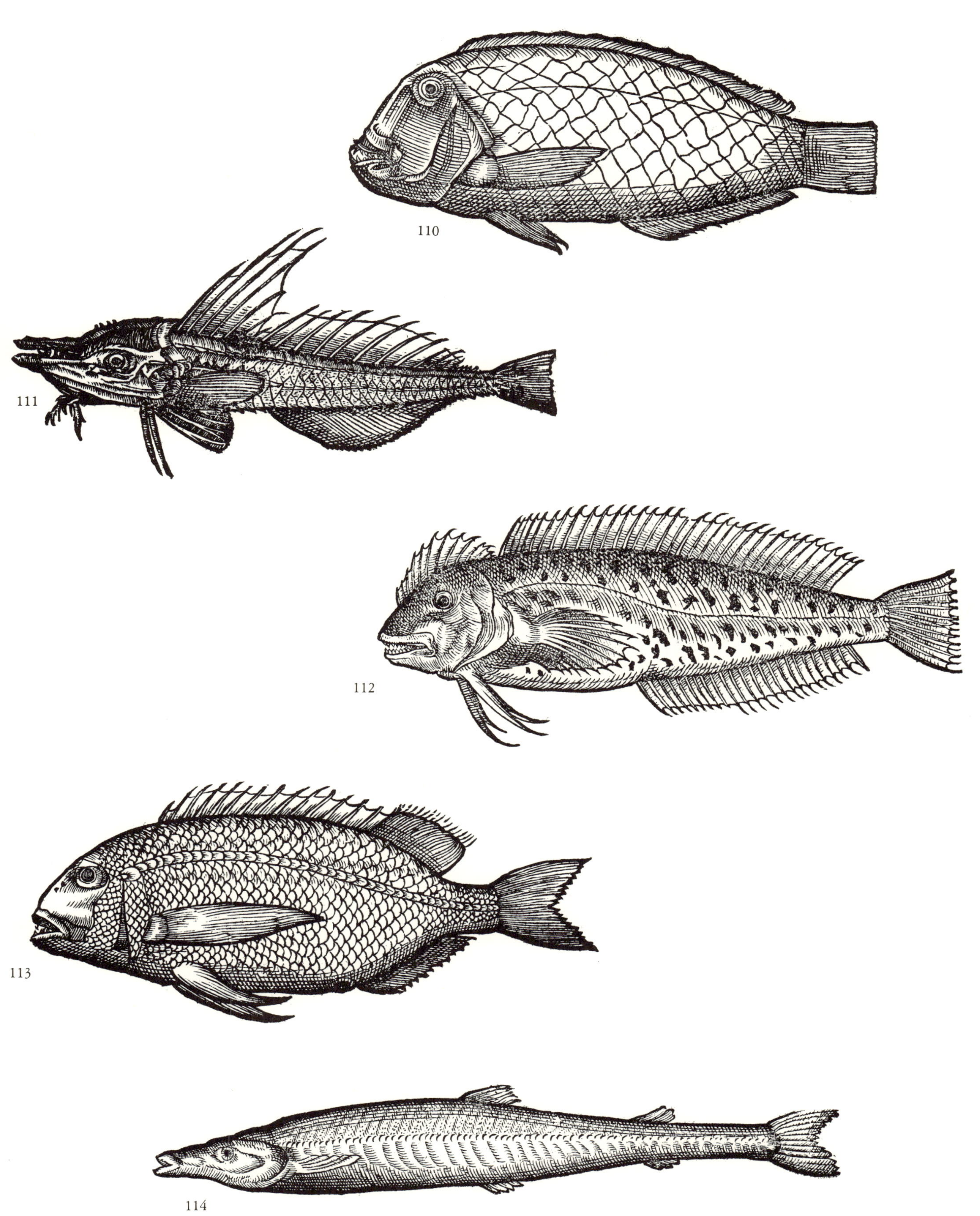

110. Razor fish. 111. A type of sea robin. 112. An unidentified fish of rocky shores (Latin, *exocoetus*).
113. Dentex (a type of sea bream). 114. Sand-eel or -launce.

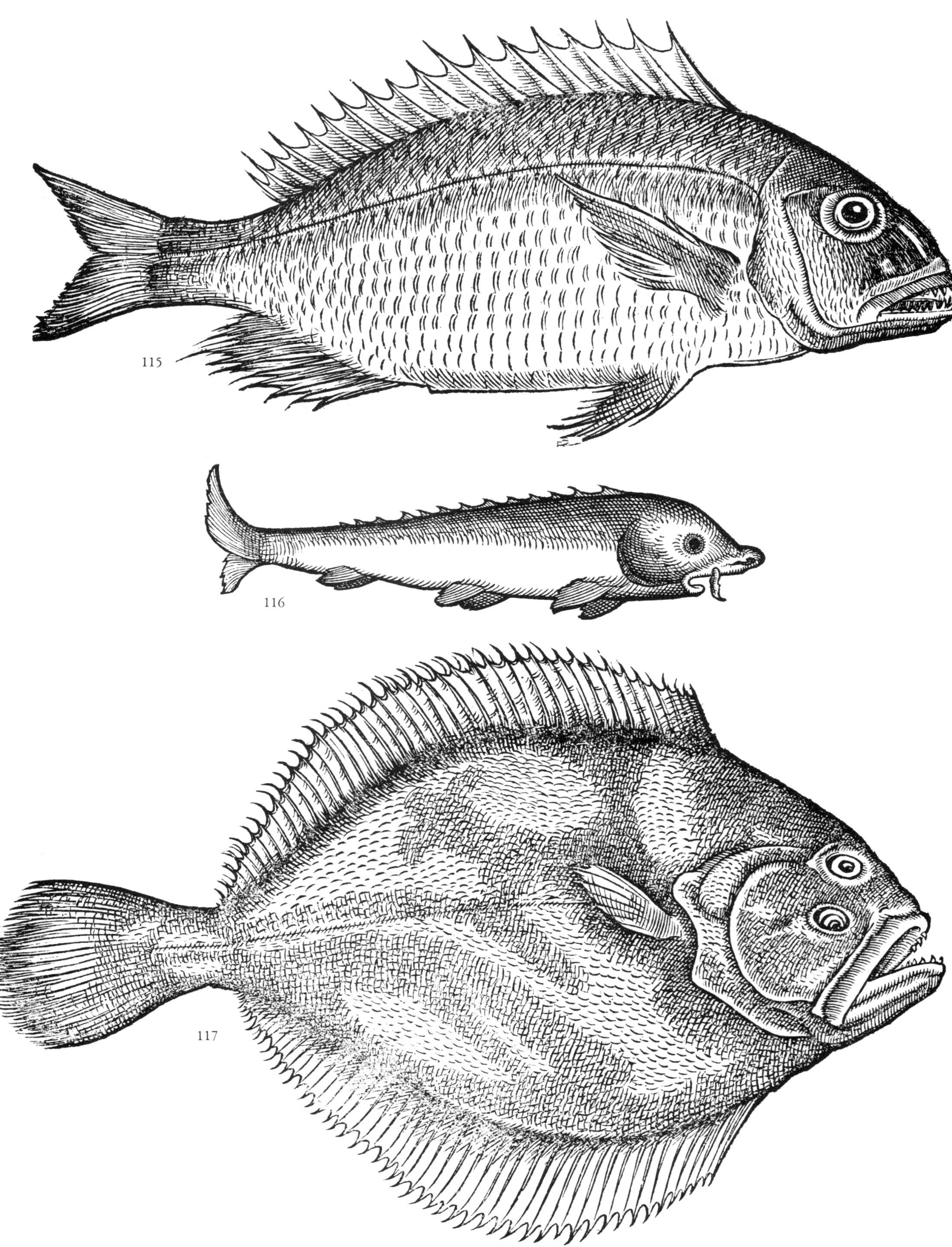

115. Another dentex. 116. Sturgeon. 117. A type of flatfish.

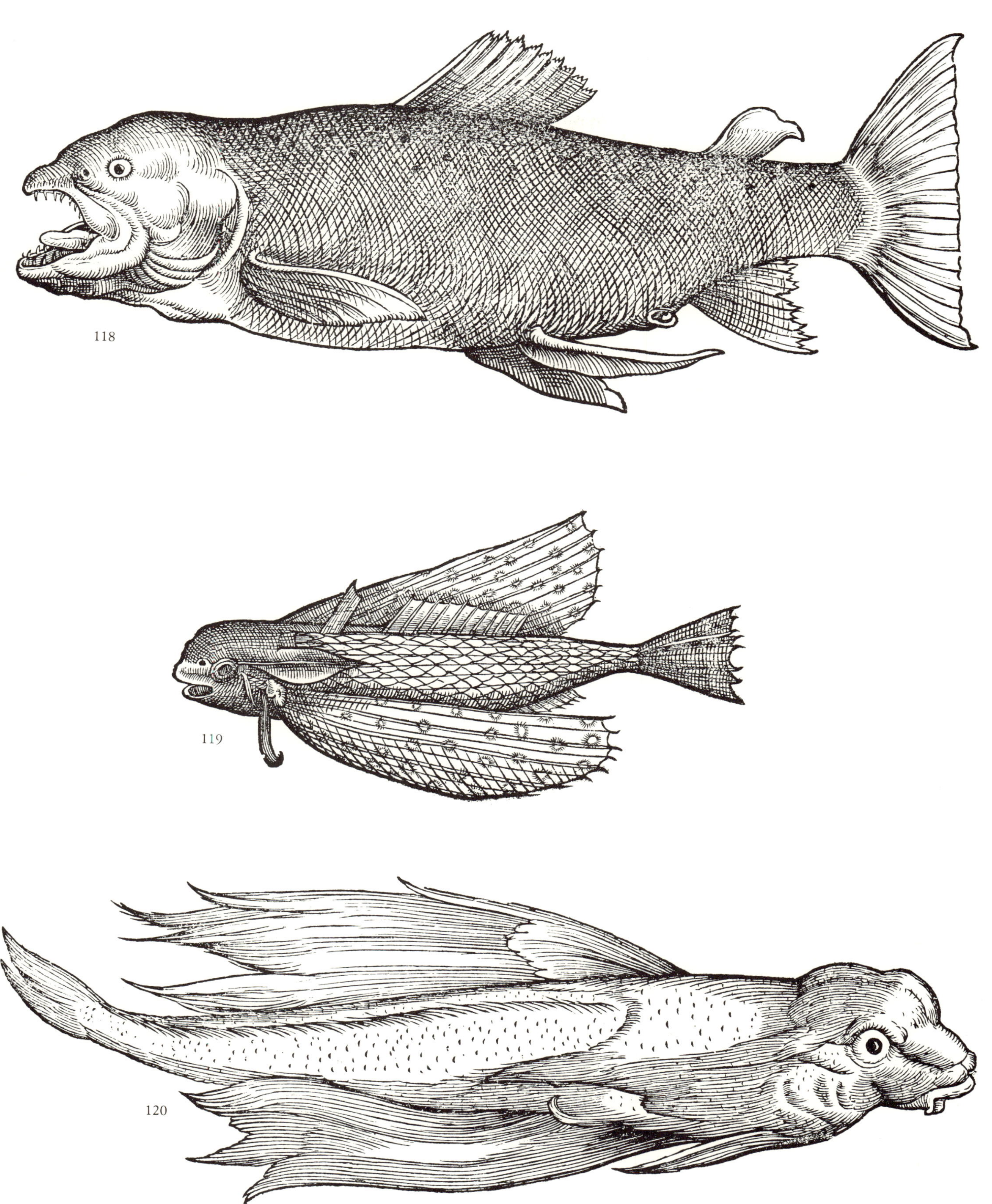

118. Salmon. 119. A type of gurnard. 120. Flying gurnard.

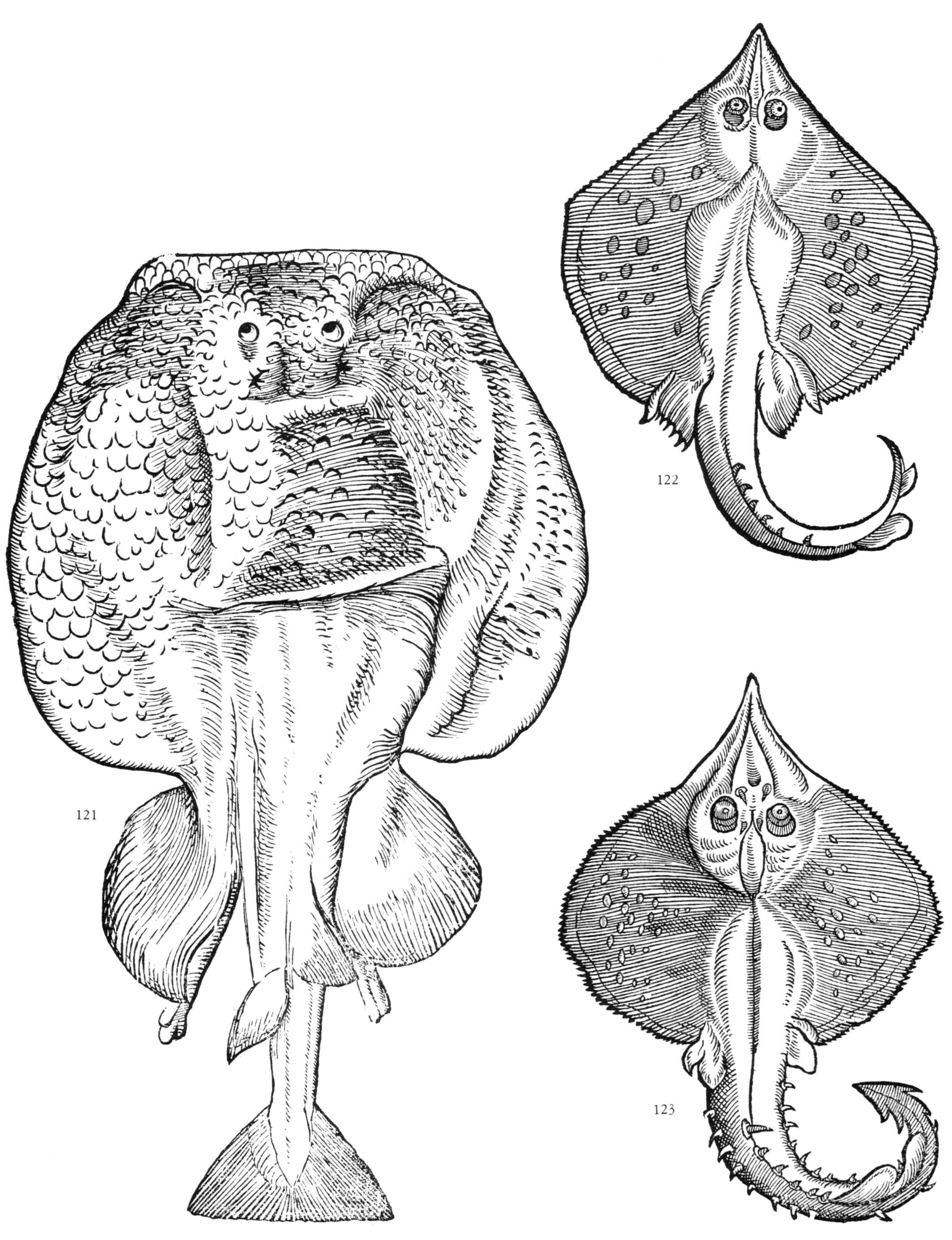

121. Electric ray. 122 and 123. Types of ray or skate.

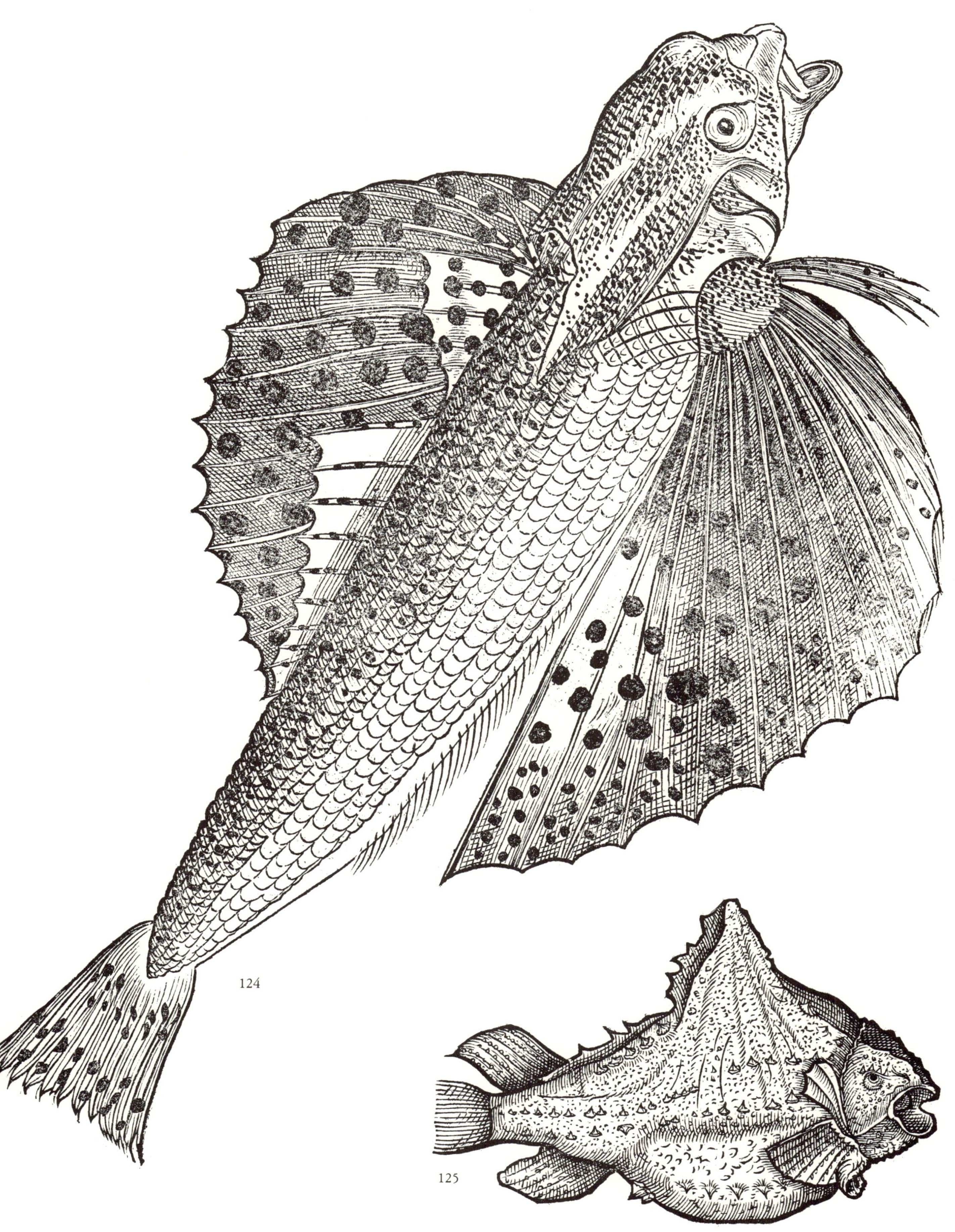

124. Flying gurnard. 125. A type of lumpfish.

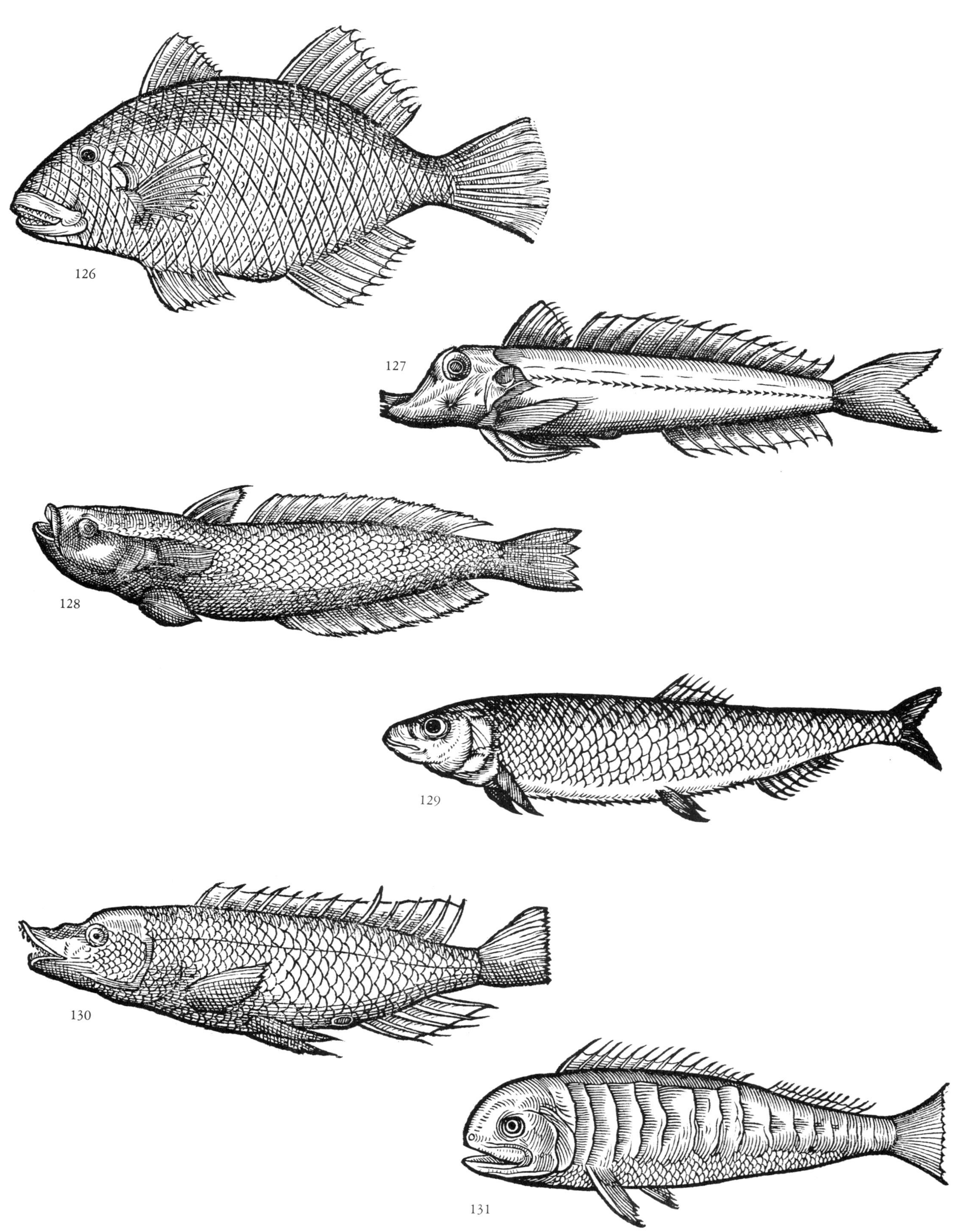

126. An unidentified fish (Latin, *aper*; German, *Geissbrachsme*). 127. A type of gurnard. 128. A type of goby. 129. Herring. 130. A type of wrasse. 131. An American trunkfish.

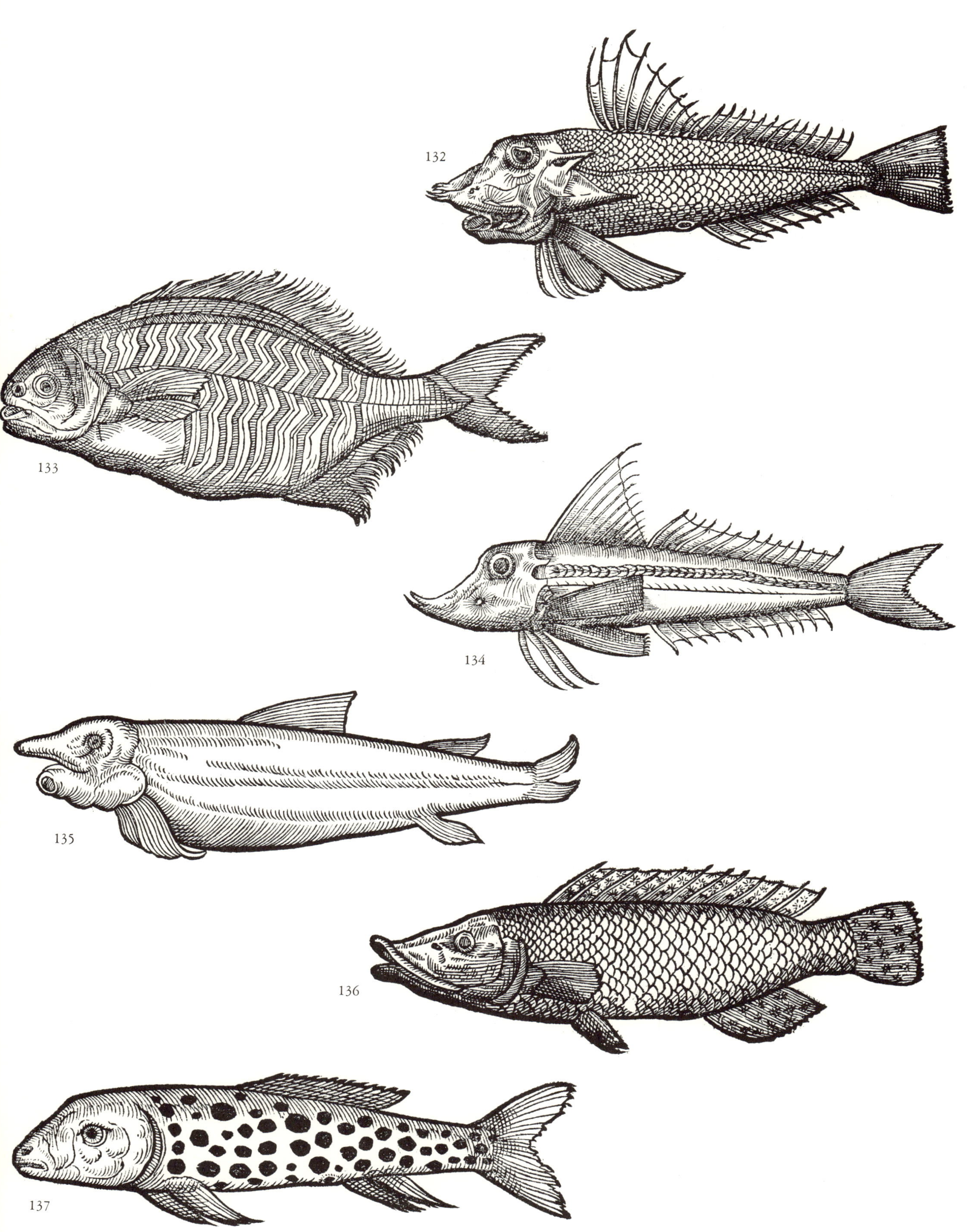

132. Sea robin. 133. An unidentified fish (Latin, *fiatola*). 134. Another member of the sea robin family. 135. Sturgeon. 136. A type of wrasse. 137. "A wonderful fish found near Lynne, England in 1555."

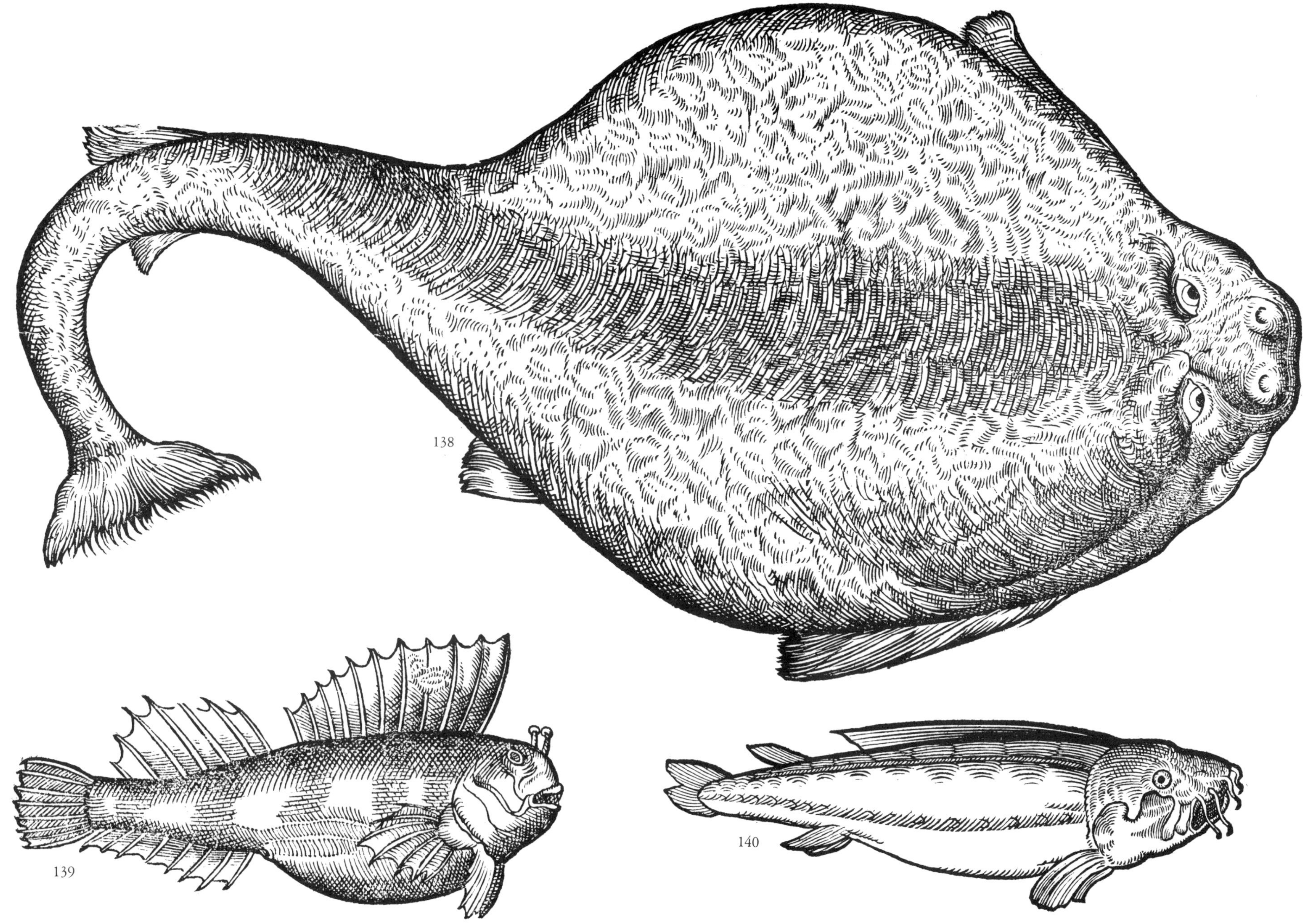

138. A type of skate or ray. 139. A type of blenny. 140. Sturgeon.

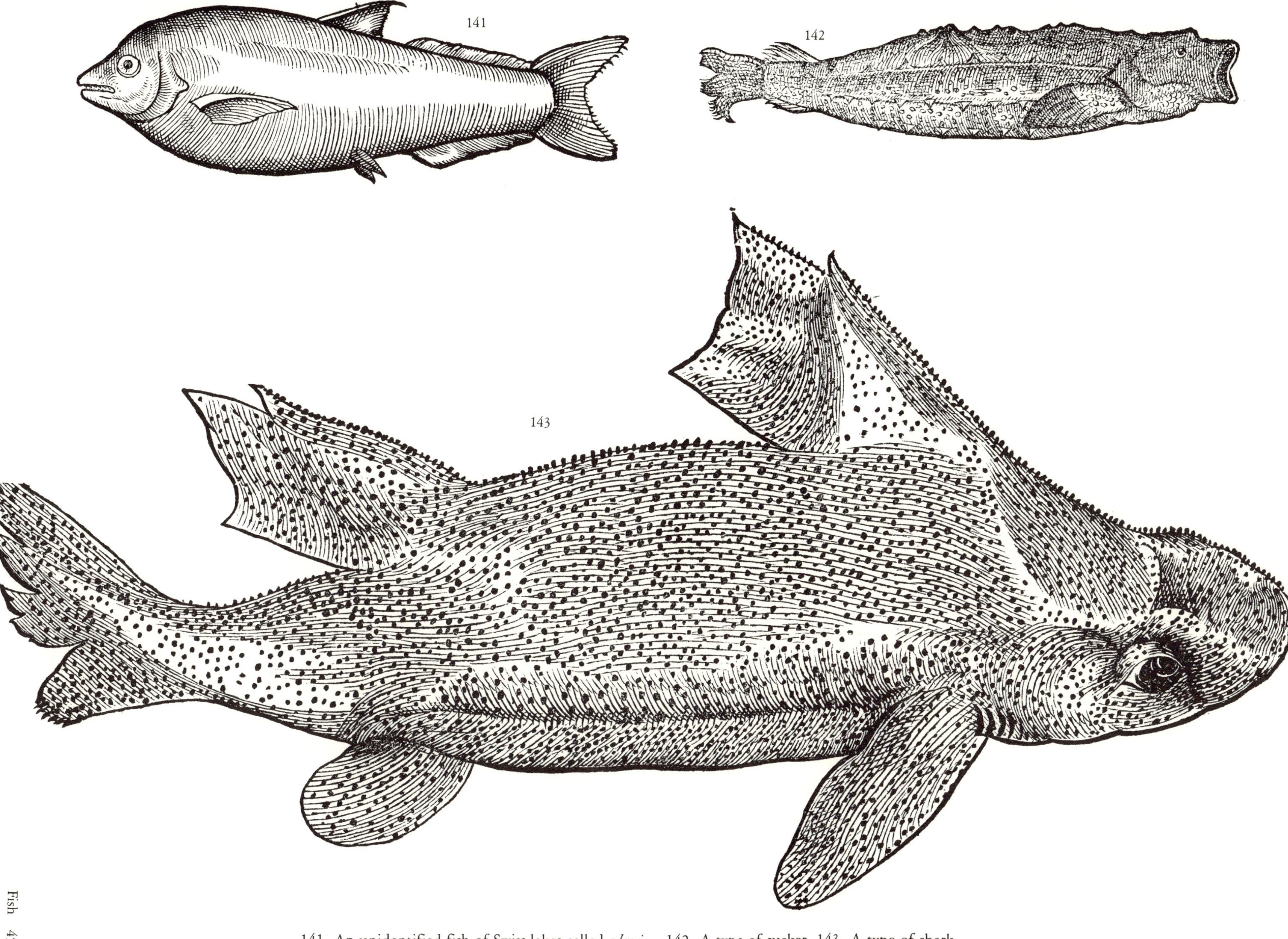

141. An unidentified fish of Swiss lakes called *glanis*. 142. A type of sucker. 143. A type of shark.

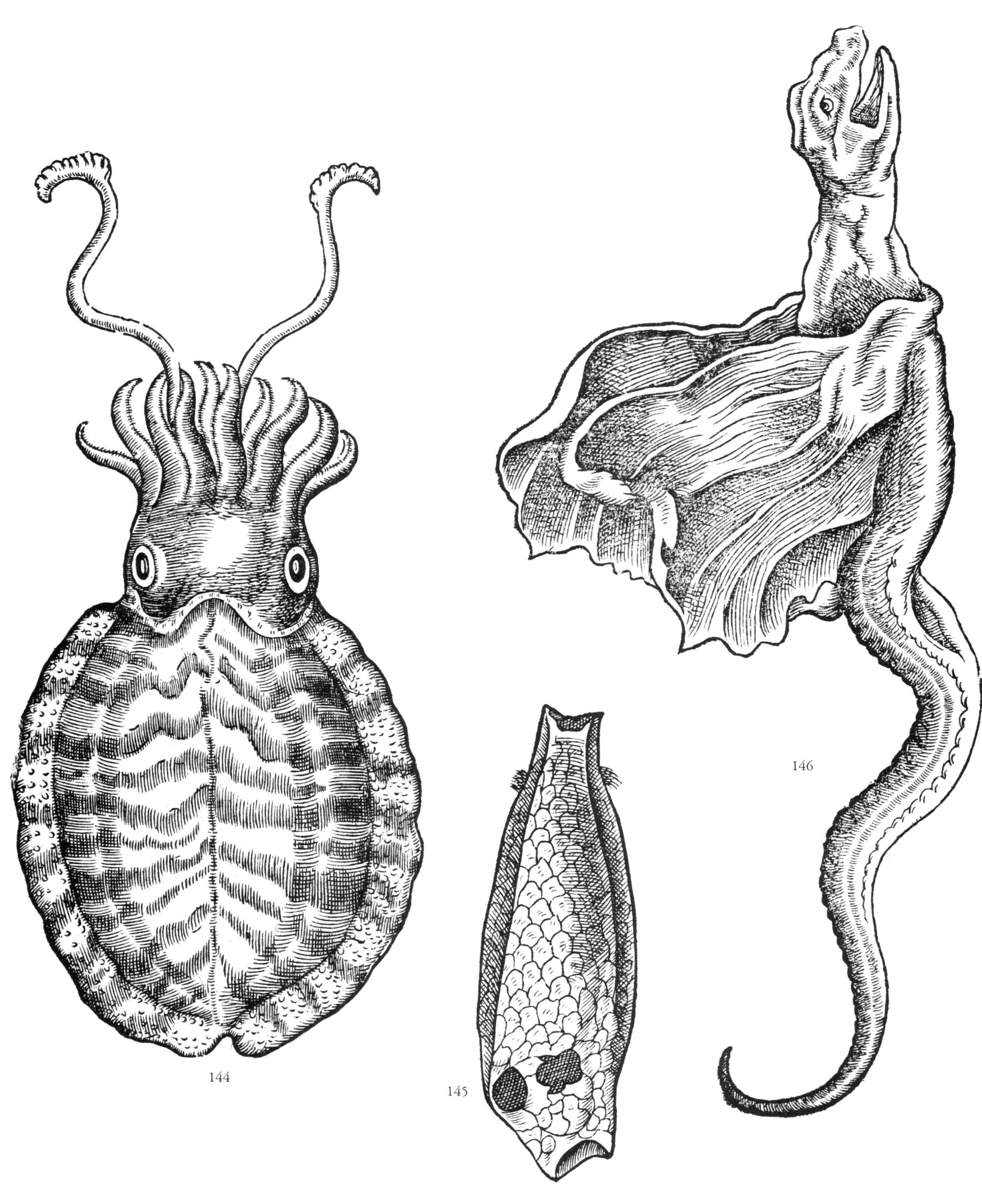

144. Squid. 145. Skeleton of a trunkfish. 146. Jenny Haniver: a mutilated ray or skate.

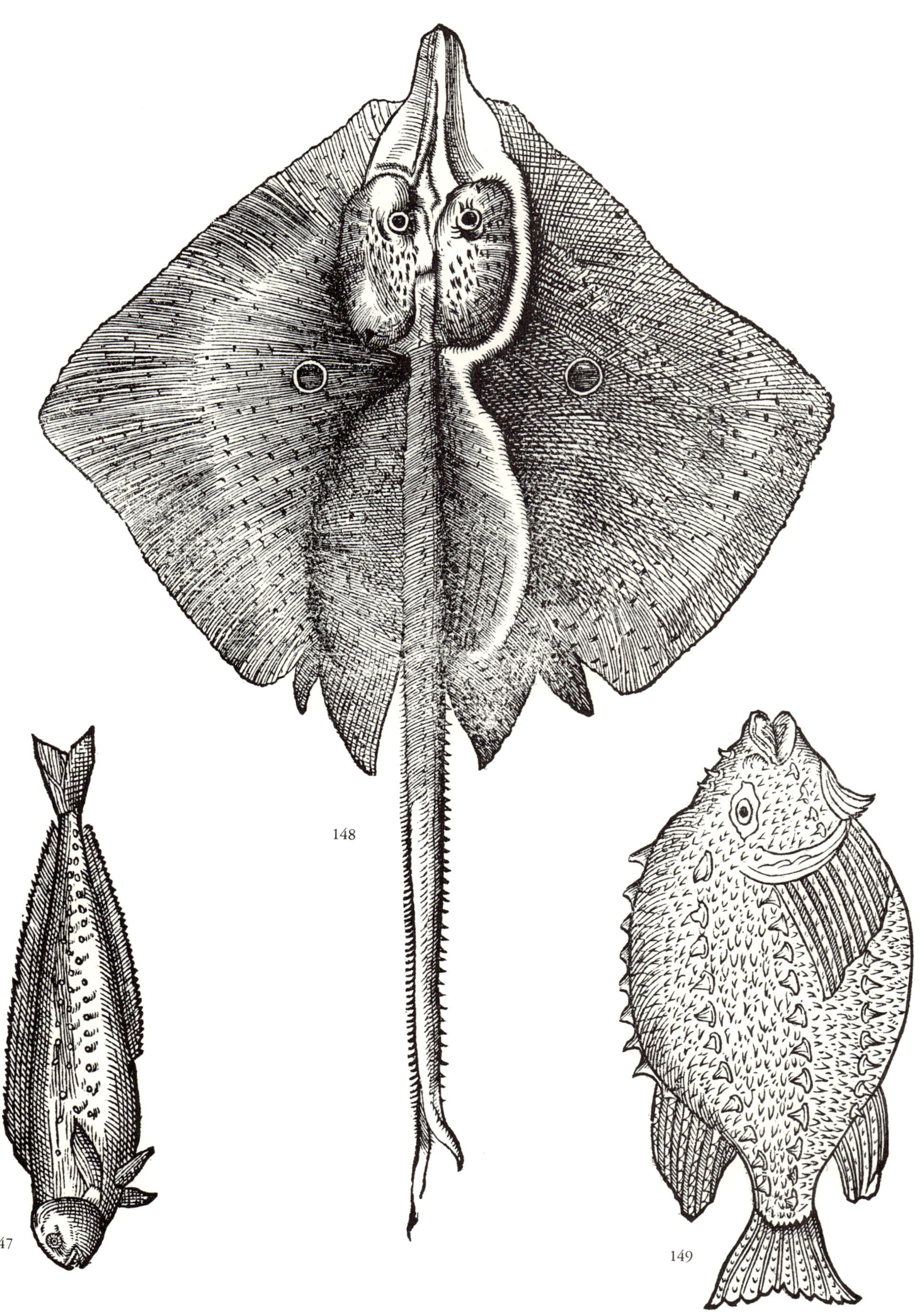

147. A type of blenny. 148. Homelyn ray. 149. Lumpsucker.

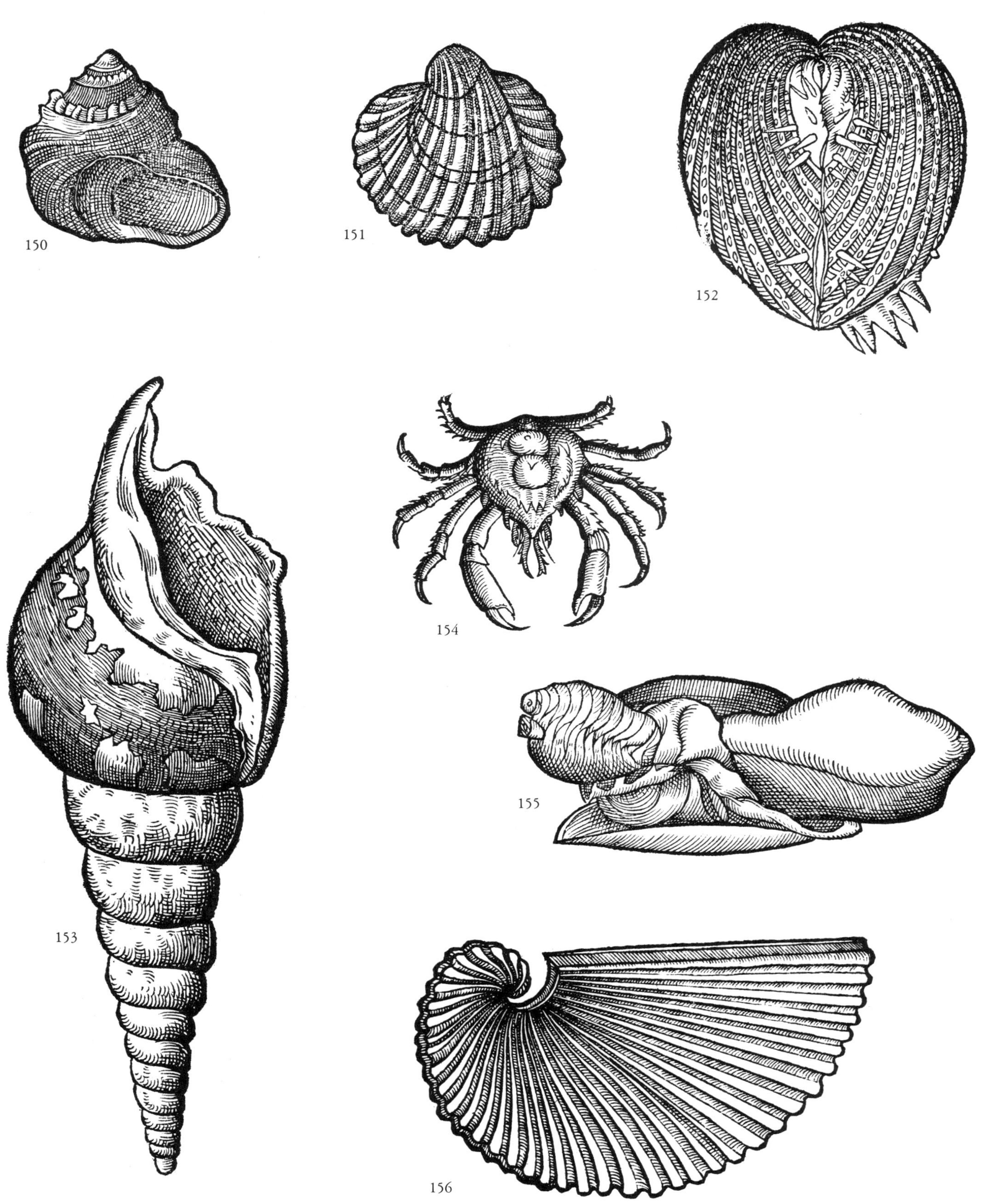

150. A type of sea snail. 151. A type of cockle. 152. Spiny cockle. 153. A large sea snail, perhaps a triton. 154. A type of crab. 155. A clam, showing internal organs. 156. Shell of paper nautilus.

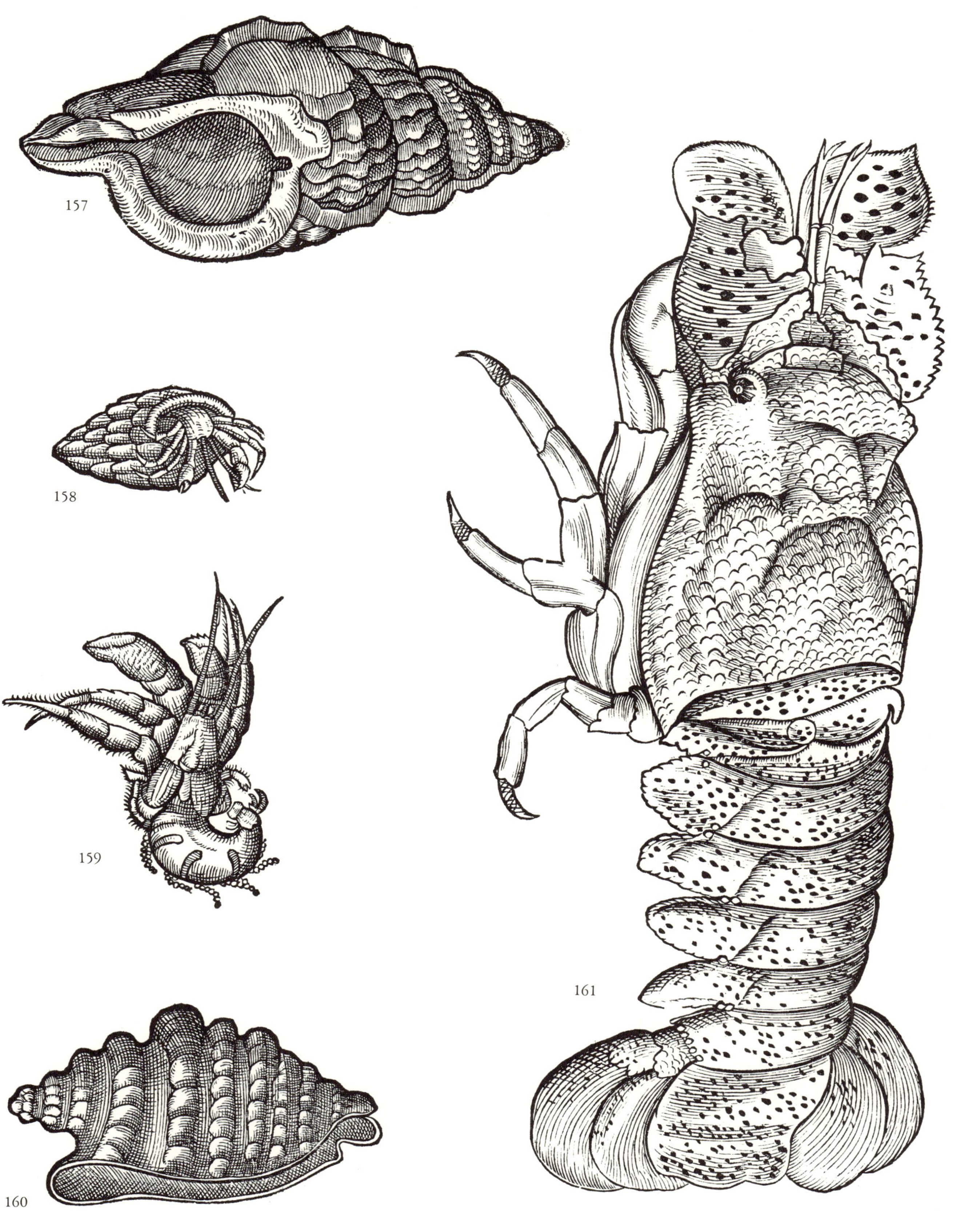

157. Rock shell, probably the source of Tyrian purple dye. 158. Hermit crab in a snail shell. 159. Naked hermit crab. 160. A sea snail resembling a helmet shell. 161. Lobster.

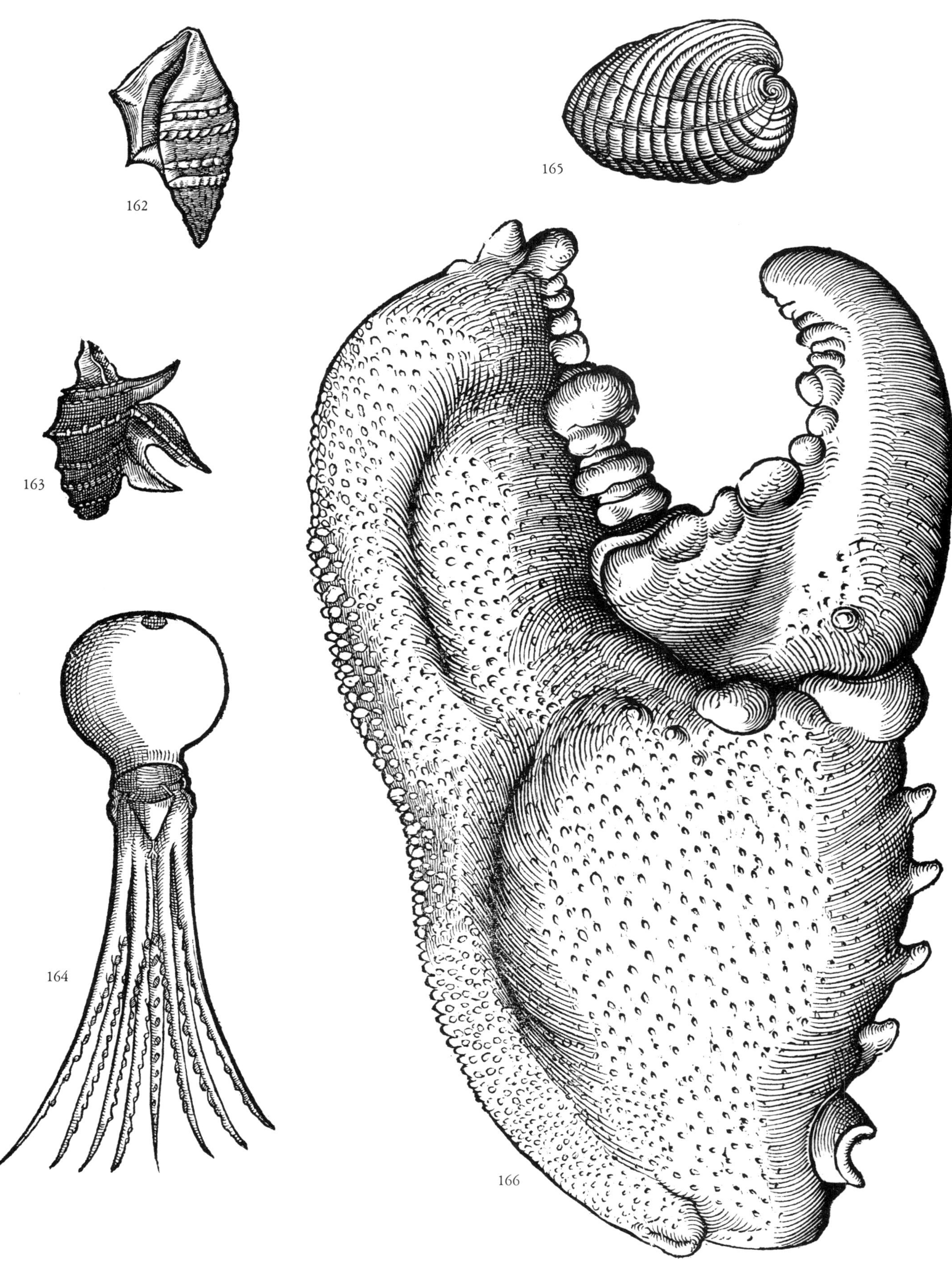

162. "Eared" sea snail. 163. Pelican's foot. 164. A type of octopus or squid. 165. A type of cockle. 166. Lobster claw.

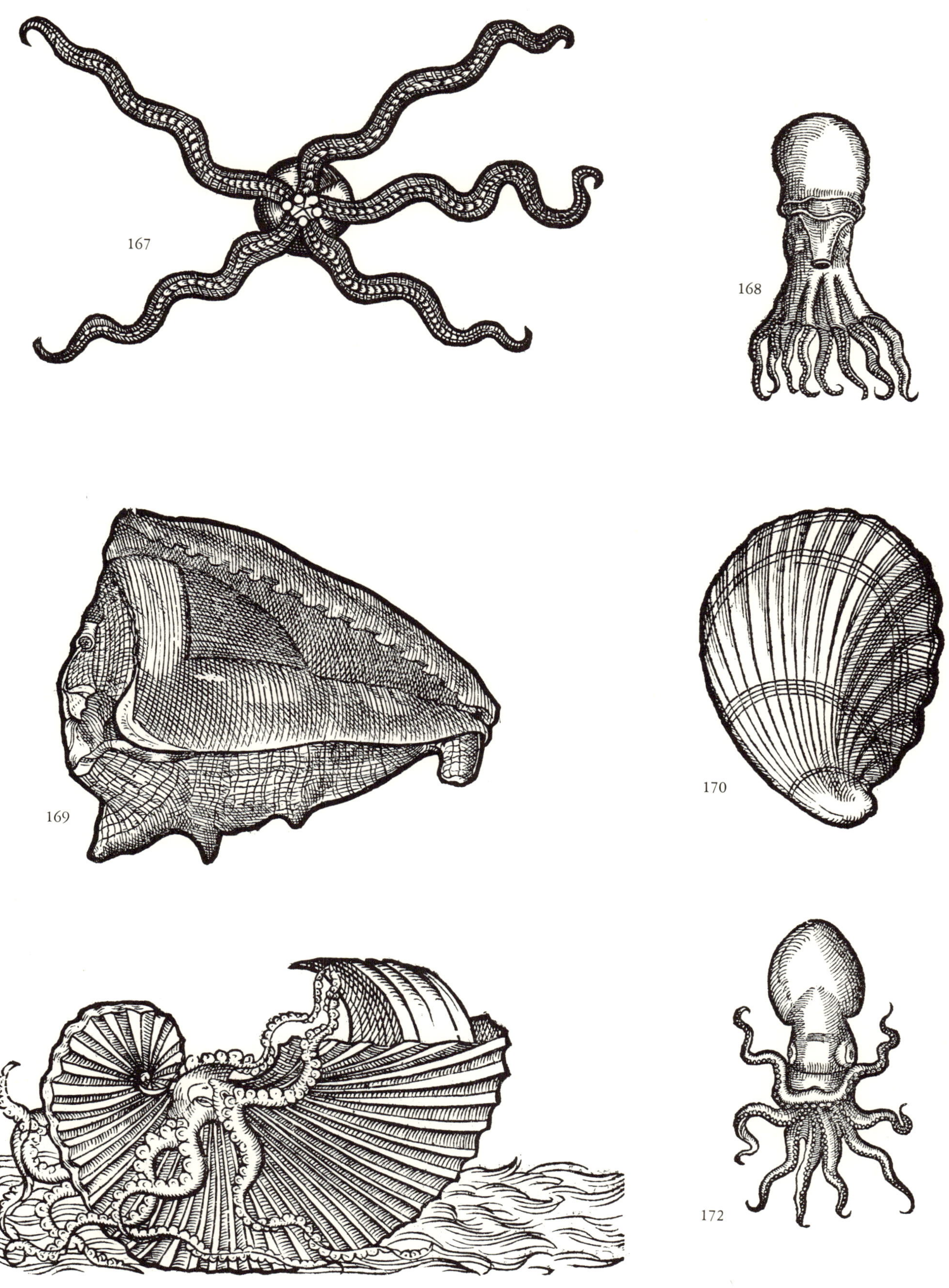

167. Serpent-star. 168. Octopus (back view). 169. A type of sea snail. 170. A type of cockle.
171. Paper nautilus. 172. Octopus (front view).

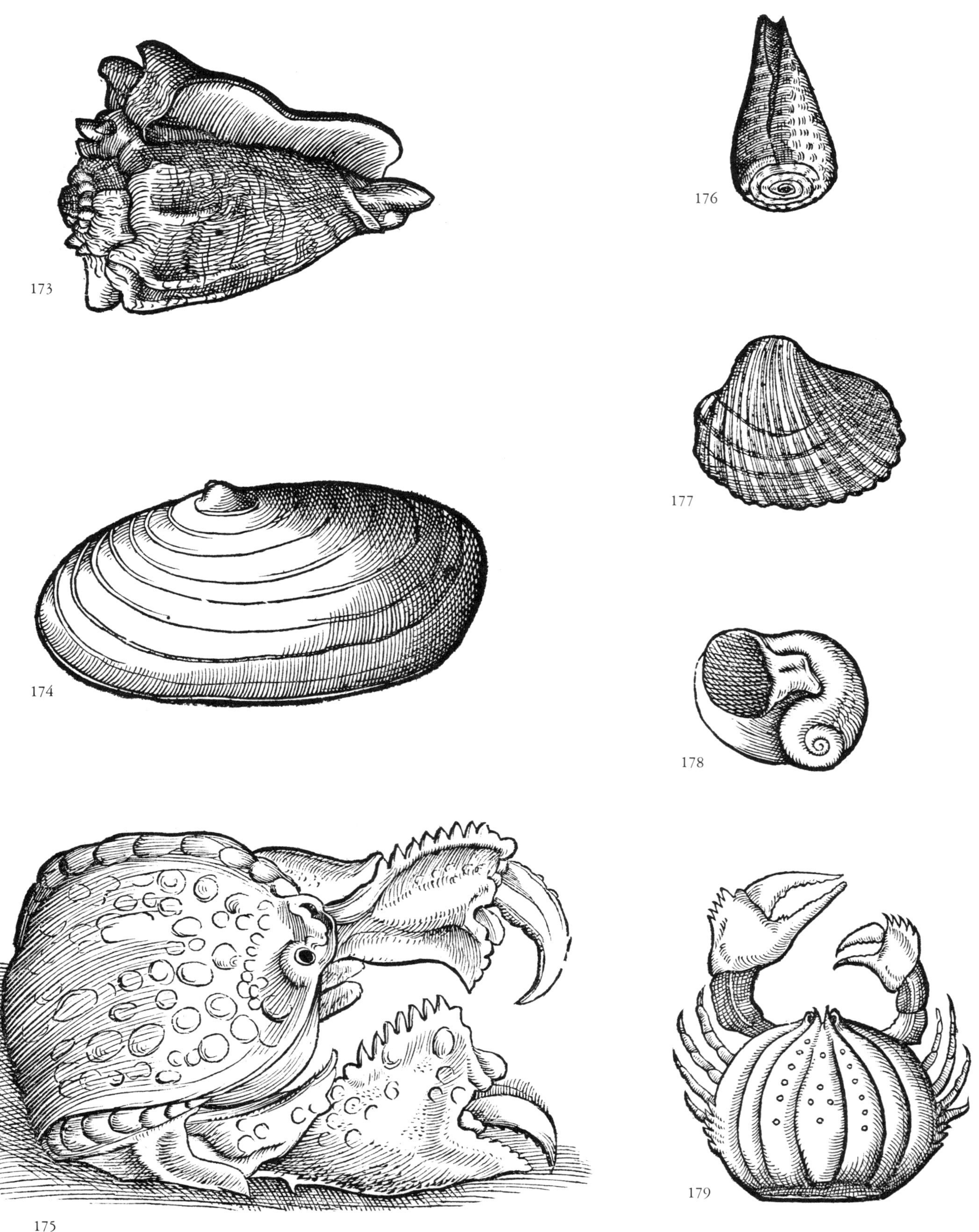

173. A type of sea snail. 174. Clam. 175. A type of crab. 176. A type of sea snail, perhaps an olive shell. 177. A type of cockle. 178. A type of sea snail. 179. A type of crab.

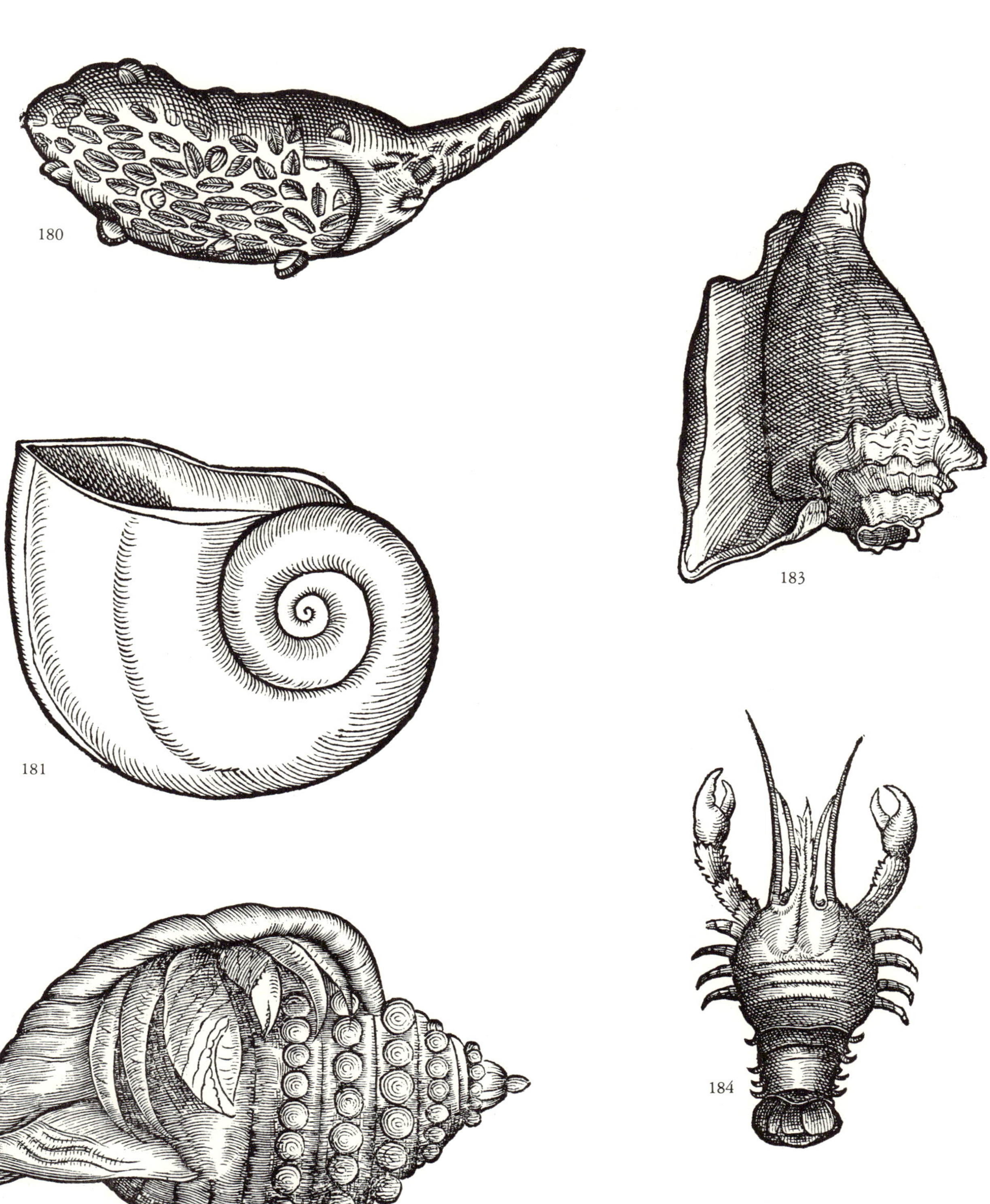

180. "Sea grape" (perhaps a sea slug). 181. A type of sea snail. 182. Hermit crab in a whelk shell. 183. Another type of sea snail. 184. A small marine crustacean.

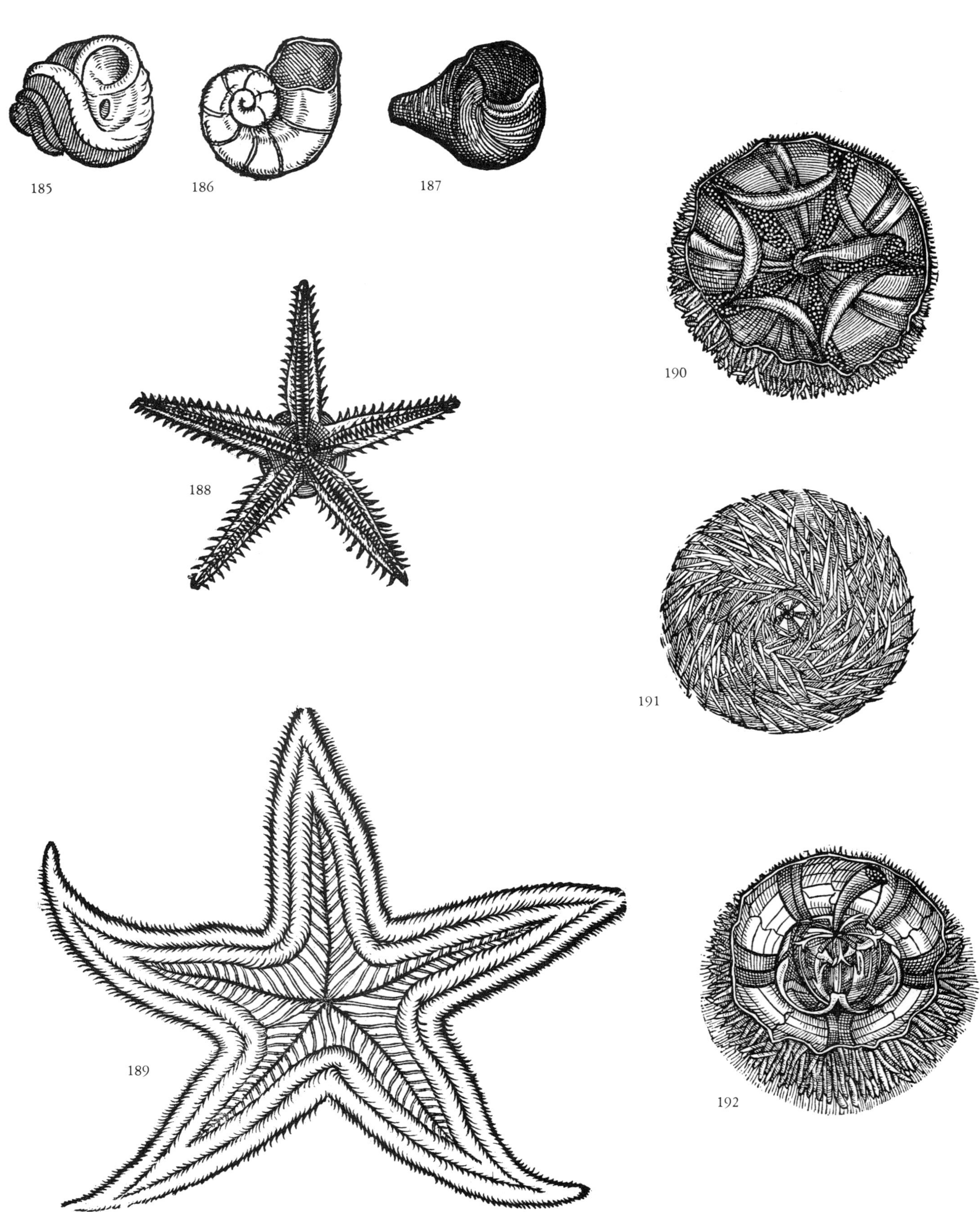

185–187. Sea snails. 188 and 189. Starfish. 190–192. Sea urchins, two of them dissected.

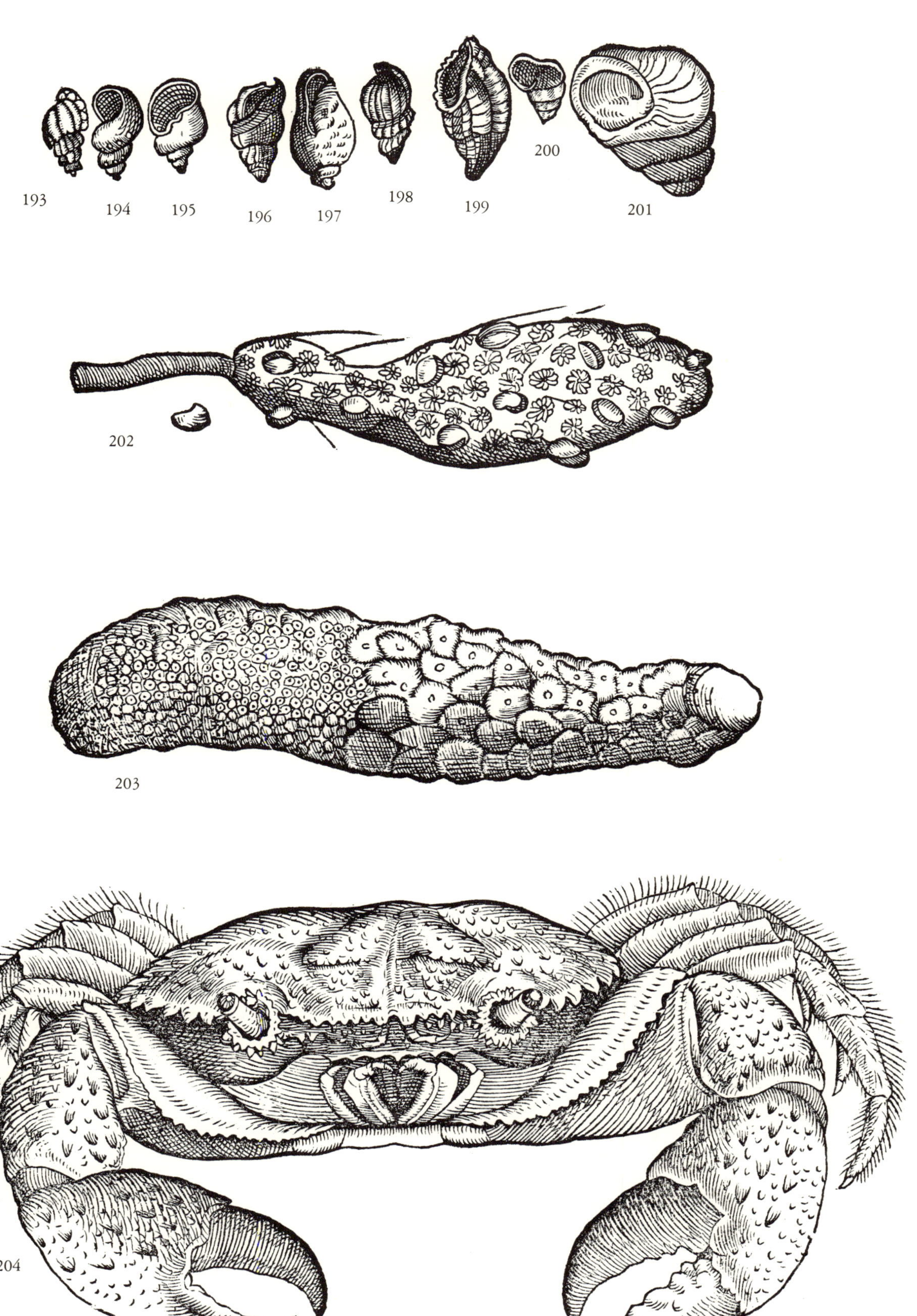

193–201. Various small sea snails. 202. Another view of the "sea grape." 203. Sea cucumber. 204. A type of crab.

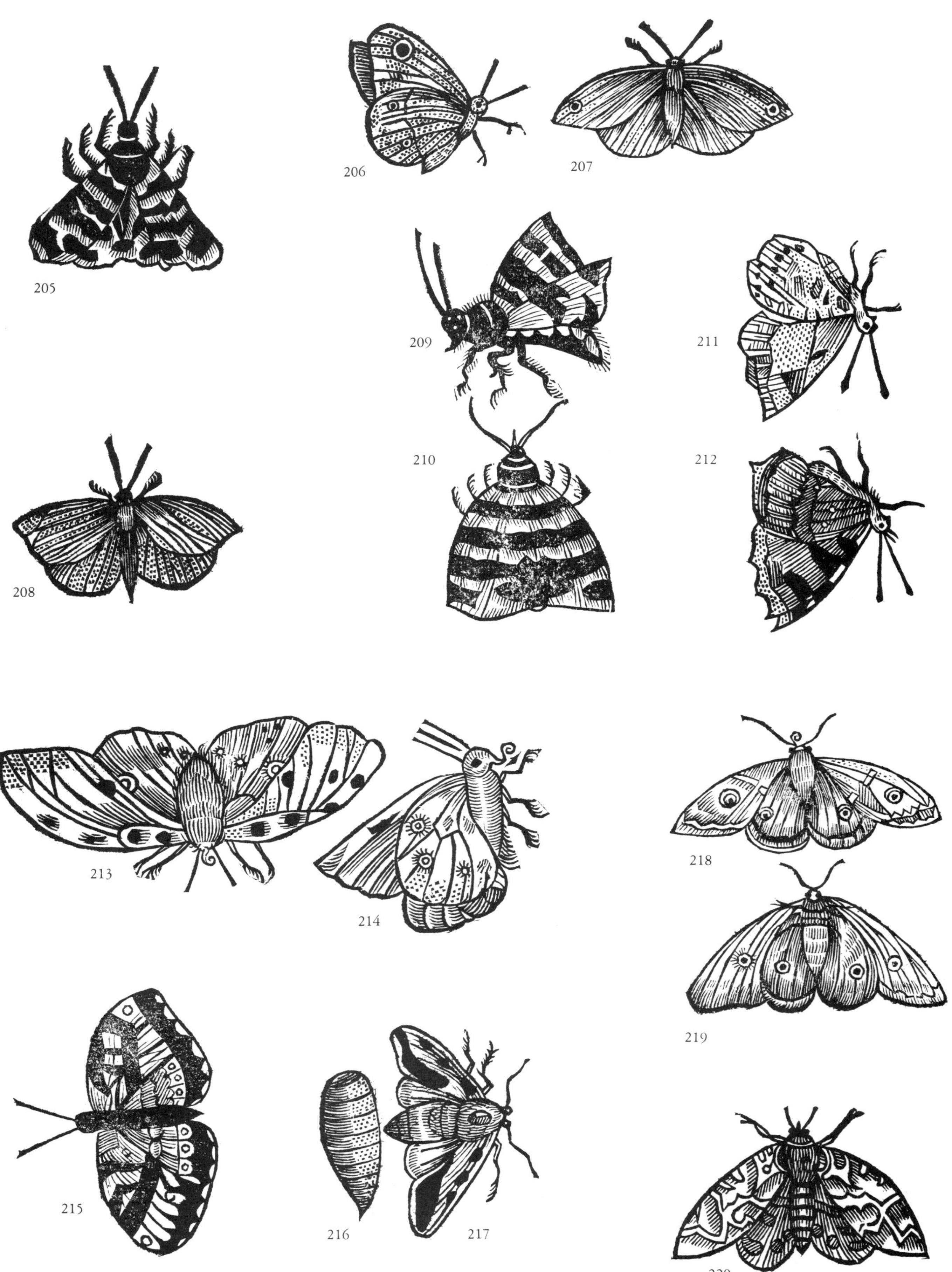

205–220. Various butterflies and moths (216: pupa).

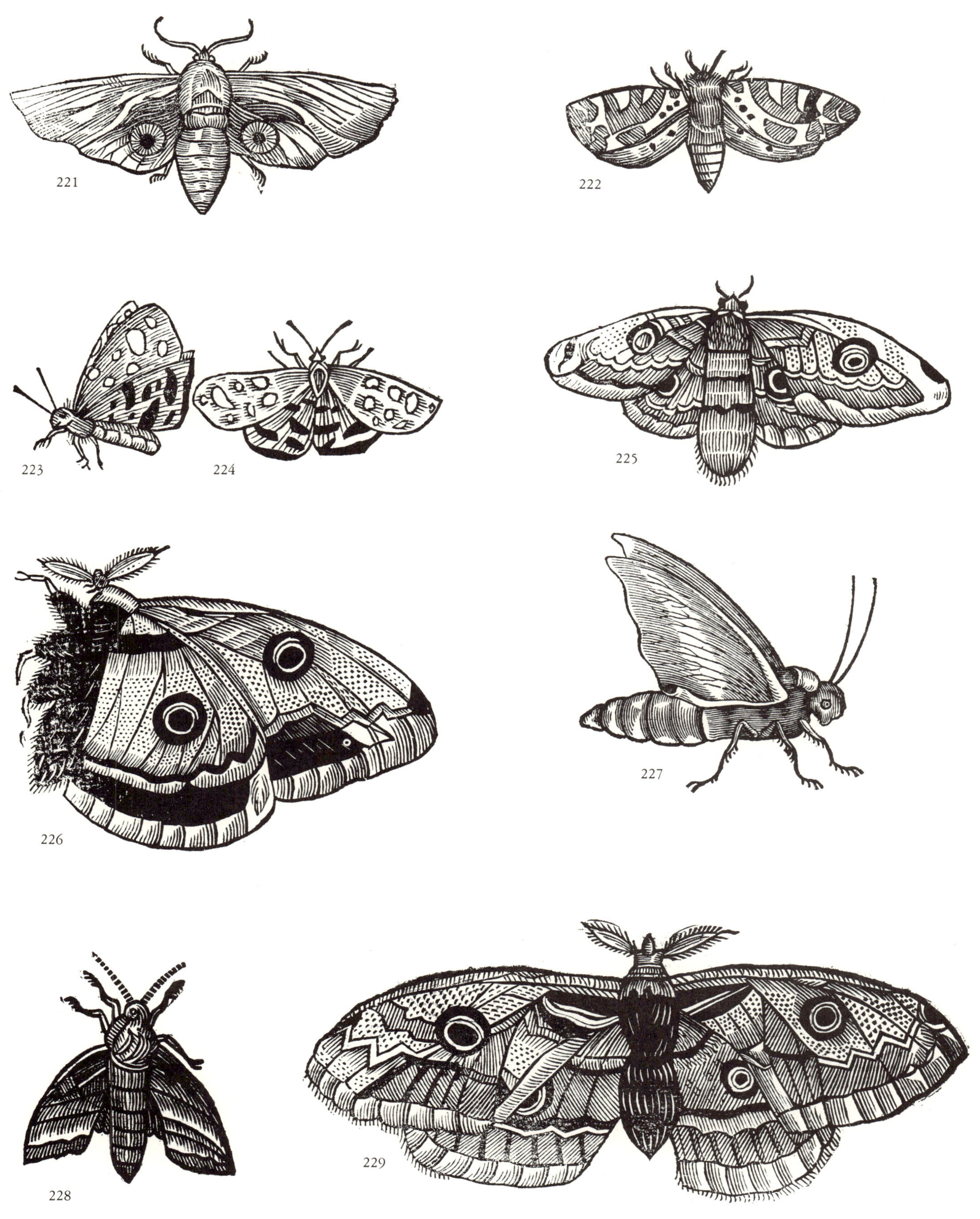

221–229. Various butterflies and moths.

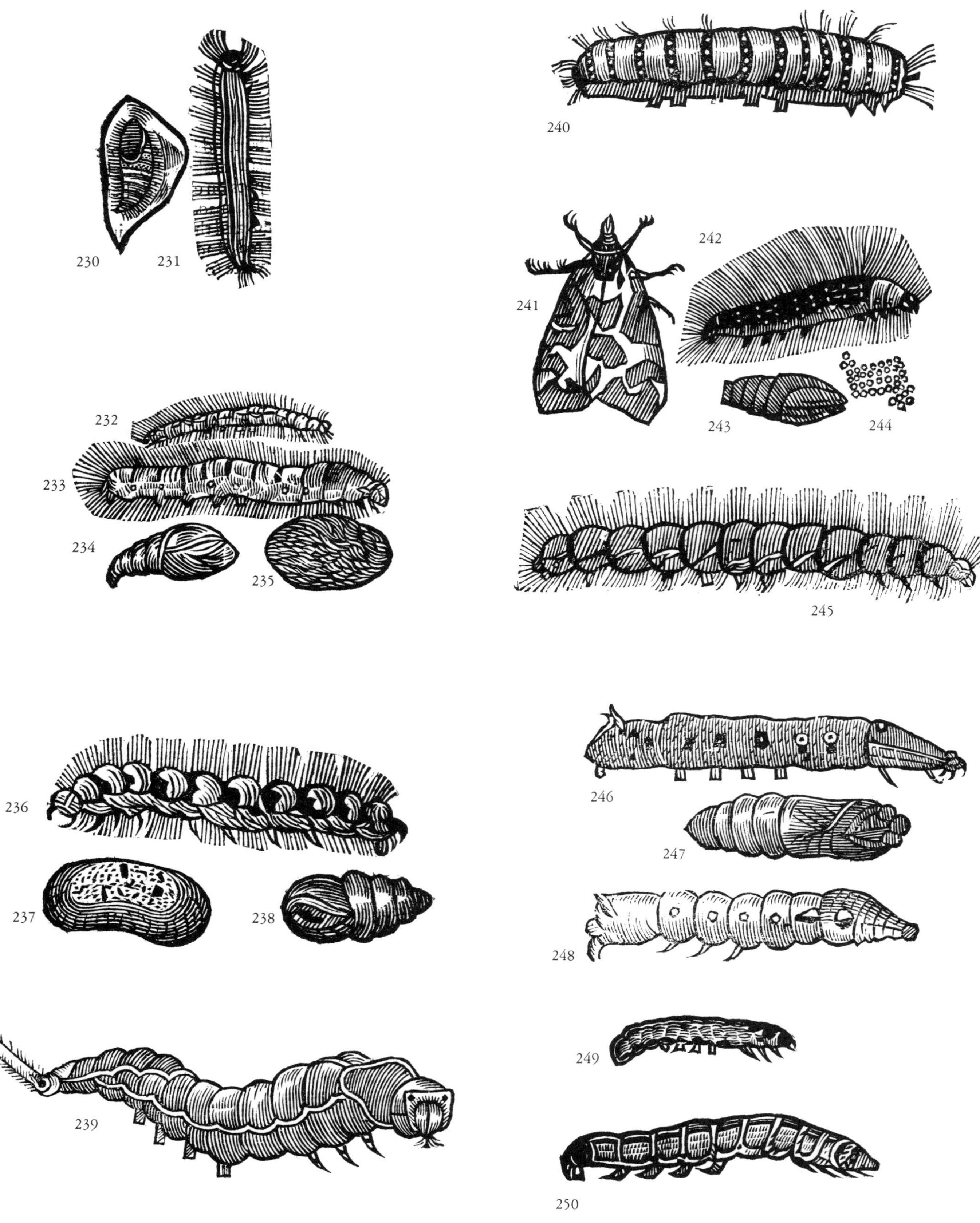

230, 234, 235, 237, 238, 243, 247. Pupae. 231–233, 236, 239, 240, 242, 245, 246, 248–250. Caterpillars or larvae. 241. A type of moth. 244. Moth eggs.

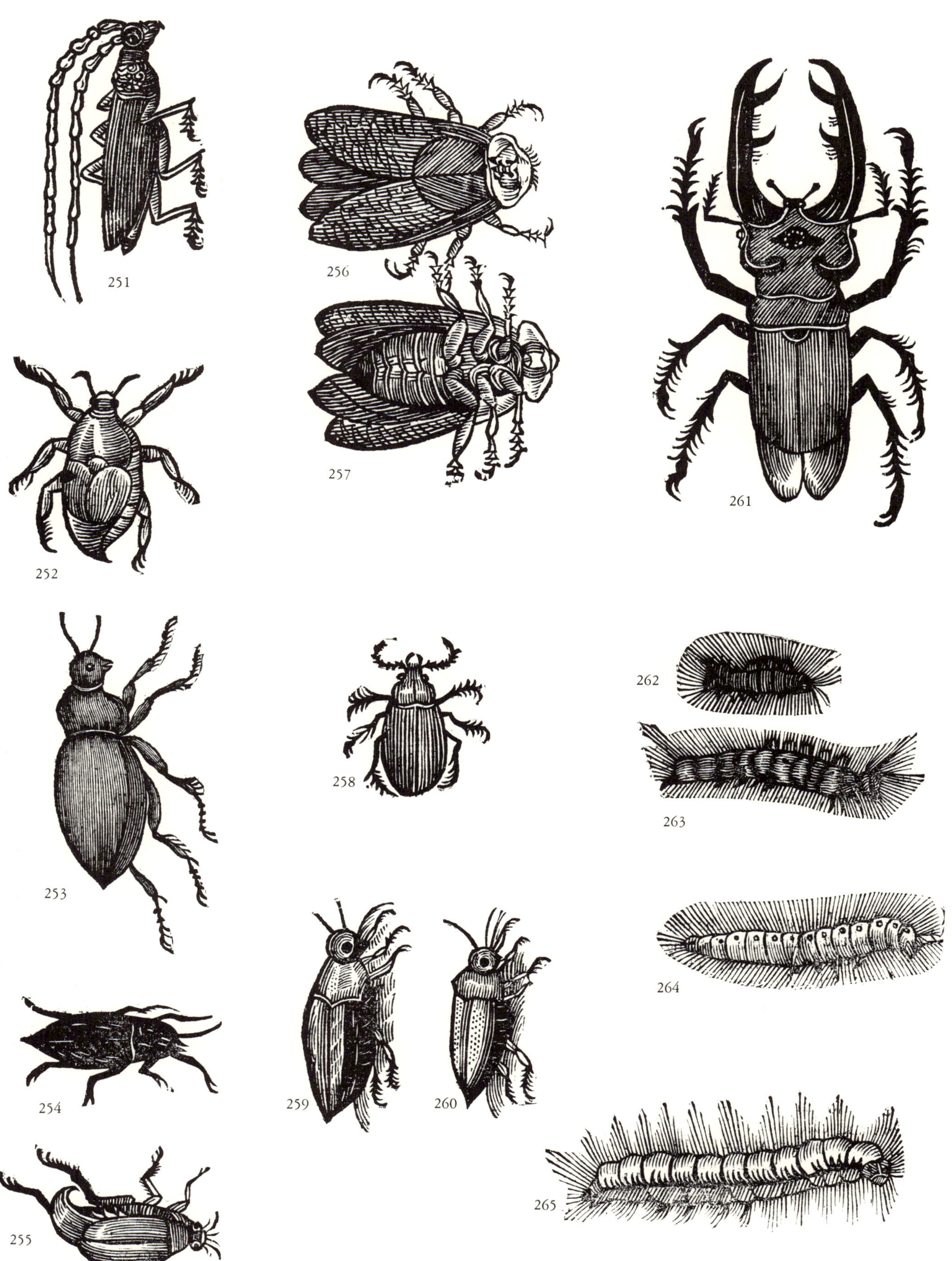

251. Longhorn or capricorn beetle. 252. A type of dung beetle. 253. A type of beetle from Constantinople. 254. Another type of beetle. 255. Dorbeetle (kin of the American June beetle). 256 and 257. Cicadas ("grashoppers"). 258–260. Various beetles (*Melolonthe*). 261. Stag-beetle. 262–265. Various caterpillars.

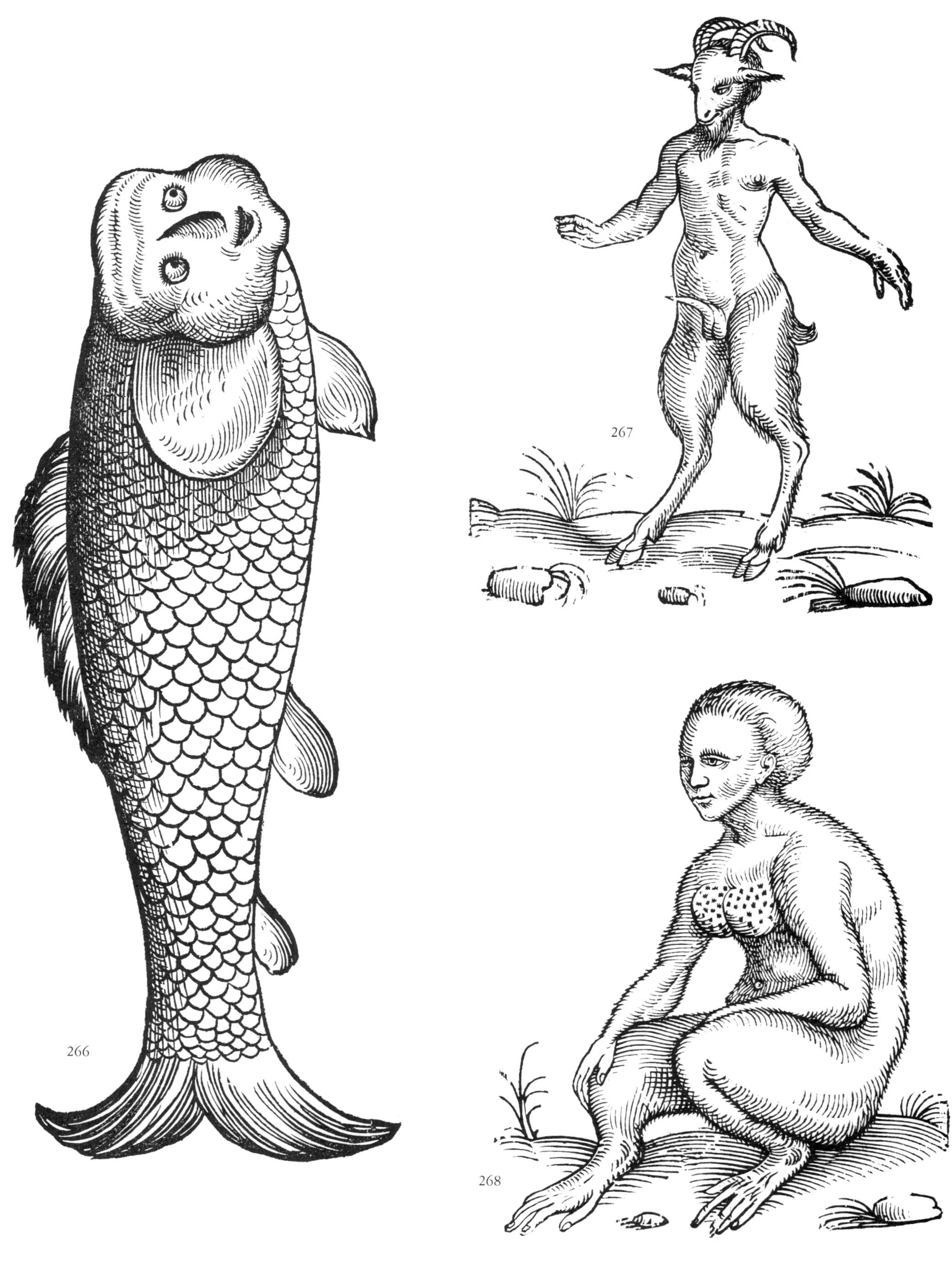

266. Carp or bream with human face, also regarded as a fanciful representation of the manatee. 267. "Aegopithecus, an Ape like a Goat." 268. Sphinx.

269

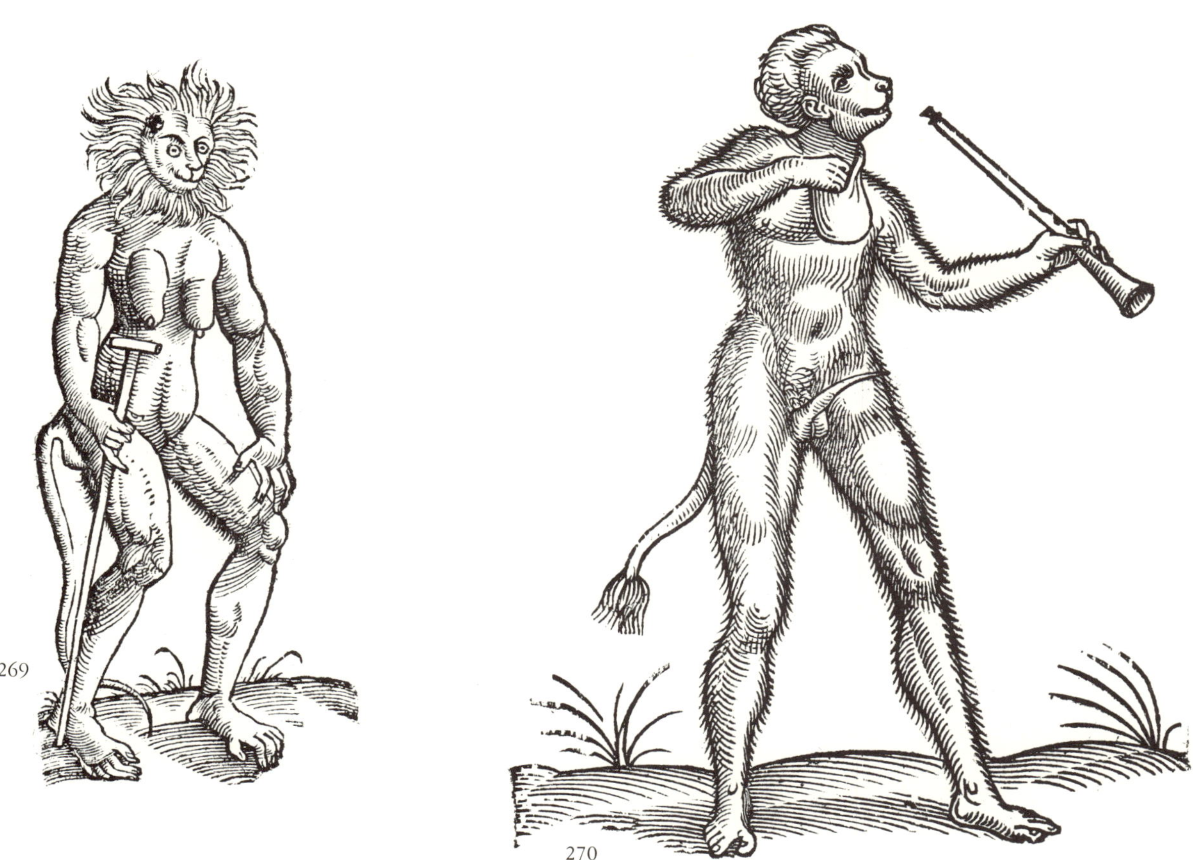

270

271

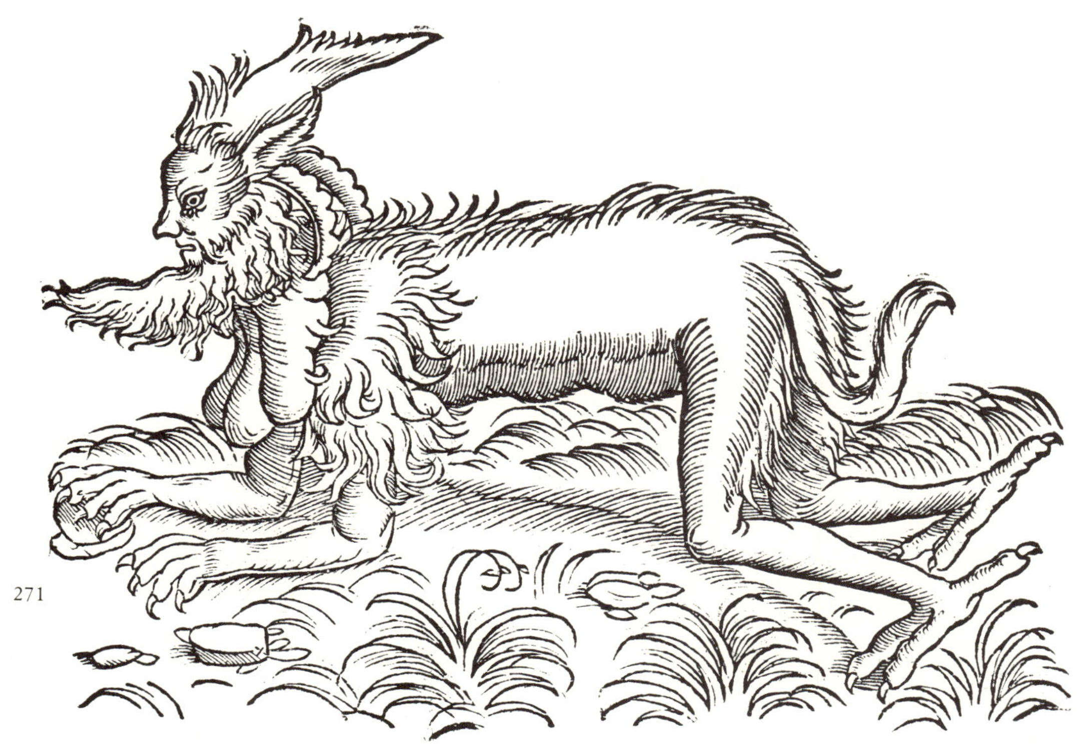

269. A maned, ape-like monster. 270. Satyr, believed to live east of India. 271. Manticora, a fierce monster allegedly caught in Saxony in 1530.

Index of Animals

The numbers are those of the illustrations.